The Hidden Places of
KENT

By
Joanna Billing

© Travel Publishing Ltd.

Published by:
Travel Publishing Ltd
7a Apollo House, Calleva Park
Aldermaston, Berks, RG7 8TN

ISBN 1-902-00739-5
© Travel Publishing Ltd

First Published:	*1993*	*Third Edition:*	*1998*
Second Edition:	*1996*	*Fourth Edition:*	*2001*

HIDDEN PLACES REGIONAL TITLES

Cambs & Lincolnshire	Chilterns
Cornwall	Derbyshire
Devon	Dorset, Hants & Isle of Wight
East Anglia	Gloucestershire & Wiltshire
Heart of England	Hereford, Worcs & Shropshire
Highlands & Islands	Kent
Lake District & Cumbria	Lancashire & Cheshire
Lincolnshire	Northumberland & Durham
Somerset	Sussex
Thames Valley	Yorkshire

HIDDEN PLACES NATIONAL TITLES

England	Ireland
Scotland	Wales

Printing by: Scotprint, Haddington
Maps by: © Maps in Minutes ™ (2000)
Editor: Joanna Billing
Cover Design: Lines & Words, Aldermaston
Cover Photographs: Tenterden; Oast Houses, Lamberhurst; St Mary's Bay
© www.britainonview.com

Foreword

The Hidden Places is a collection of easy to use travel guides taking you, in this instance, on a relaxed but informative tour of Kent. Traditionally referred to as "The Garden of England", it offers the visitor a very attractive landscape of rolling woodland, remote marshlands, orchards, hop fields and an extensive coastline full of character. The county also contains idyllic rural villages, imposing castles and palaces and is home to countless ancient buildings including, of course, the glorious Canterbury Cathedral founded in the 6th century. Combine these attractions with Kent's heritage which has its origins in Saxon, Norman and Roman times, its fascinating maritime history and of course its countless literary connections, there are very compelling reasons for spending time exploring this attractive county.

This edition of *The Hidden Places of Kent* is published *in full colour.* All *Hidden Places* titles will now be published in colour which will ensure that readers can properly appreciate the attractive scenery and impressive places of interest in this county and, of course, in the rest of the British Isles. We do hope that you like the new format.

Our books contain a wealth of interesting information on the history, the countryside, the towns and villages and the more established places of interest in the county. But they also promote the more secluded and little known visitor attractions and places to stay, eat and drink many of which are easy to miss unless you know exactly where you are going.

We include hotels, inns, restaurants, public houses, teashops, various types of accommodation, historic houses, museums, gardens, garden centres, craft centres and many other attractions throughout Kent, all of which are comprehensively indexed. Most places are accompanied by an attractive photograph and are easily located by using the map at the beginning of each chapter. We do not award merit marks or rankings but concentrate on describing the more interesting, unusual or unique features of each place with the aim of making the reader's stay in the local area an enjoyable and stimulating experience.

Whether you are visiting the area for business or pleasure or in fact are living in the county we do hope that you enjoy reading and using this book. We are always interested in what readers think of places covered (or not covered) in our guides so please do not hesitate to use the reader reaction forms provided to give us your considered comments. We also welcome any general comments which will help us improve the guides themselves. Finally if you are planning to visit any other corner of the British Isles we would like to refer you to the list of other *Hidden Places* titles to be found at the rear of the book and to the Travel Publishing website at www.travelpublishing.co.uk.

Travel Publishing

Regional Map

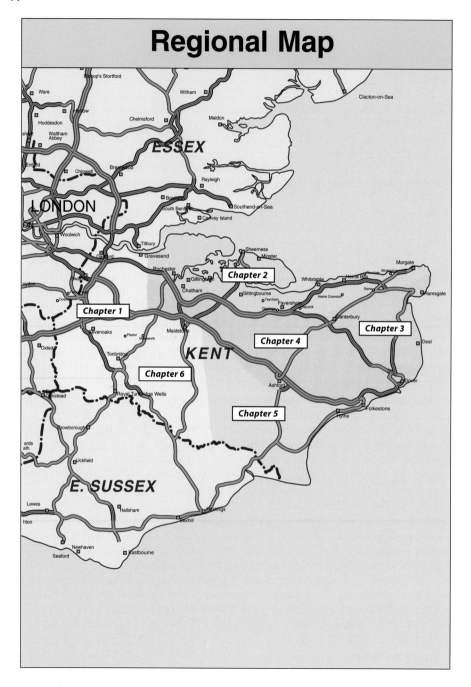

Contents

1 West Kent

This western region of Kent, that lies so close to the spreading suburban areas of Greater London has still managed to maintain an identity that is all its own. Along with the glorious countryside, the maritime heritage along the banks of the River Thames and the offbeat pronunciation of the towns and villages, this area of Kent has staved off the encroachment of the metropolis.

Water dominates much of the history of Kent and so this area too. The short crossing to Europe via Dover and the Thames Estuary have always made this one of the first places to attract invaders. Prehistoric remains can be found here along with evidence of Roman occupation at Lullingstone near Eynsford and Croft Roman Villa at

Brands Hatch

Orpington. Danes and Vikings also invaded and the now picturesque village of Aylesford has, over the centuries, been witness to more than its fair share of bloodshed.

More peaceful times saw the creation of grand manor houses and the conversion of castles into more comfortable homes and this area abounds in interesting and historic places such as Cobham Hall, Knole House, Old Soar Manor, Ightham Mote, Penshurst Place and magnificent Hever Castle.

However, whilst these houses have much to offer visitors, both outside and within, two places stand out as being of particular interest. Chartwell, the home of Sir Winston and Lady Churchill from the 1920s until the great statesman's death in the 1960s, has been left just as it

Knole Park, Sevenoaks

was when the couple were still alive and it remains a lasting tribute to this extraordinary man. Meanwhile, now contained within the M25, lies Down House, the home of Charles Darwin and the place where he formulated his theories of evolution and wrote his famous work *The Origin of Species by Means of Natural Selection*.

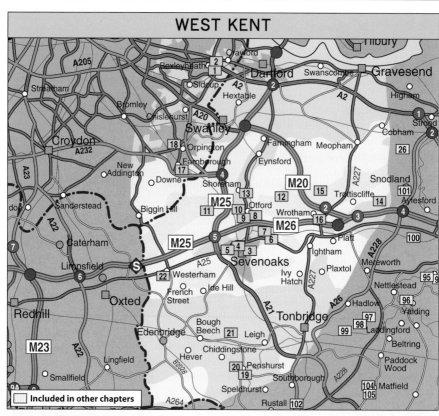

WEST KENT

© MAPS IN MINUTES ™ (2000)

PLACES TO STAY, EAT, DRINK AND SHOP

GRAVESEND

Gravesend marks the point at which ships entering the Thames, which is half a mile wide at this point, take on board a river pilot for the journey upstream, This is also where those who had died on board were unloaded before the ships entered London. A busy maritime community, with cutters and tugs helping to maintain a steady flow of river traffic, it is this, rather than the town itself, that draws visitors to Gravesend, partly because much of the town was destroyed by fire in 1727. One of the many buildings that did not survive the fire was the parish **Church of St George** and the building seen today was rebuilt after the disaster in fine Georgian style. Whilst the church is certainly attractive, it is the graveyard that is more interesting as this is thought to be the final resting place of the famous Red Indian princess, Pocahontas. The daughter of a native American chieftain, who reputedly saved the life of the English settler, John Smith, in Virginia, Pocahontas died on board ship (either from small pox, fever or tuberculosis) in 1617 whilst she was on her way back to America with her husband, John Rolfe. A life-sized statue marks her supposed burial place in the churchyard.

Another building of interest in the town, and one that did survive the 18th century fire, is 14th century **Milton Chantry**, a small building that is home to the chapel of a leper hospital and the chantry of the de Valence and Monechais families. The building later became an inn and, in 1780, part of a fort.

Despite its name, this is not a reference to Gravesend being the last resting place of poor unfortunates who died on board ship but it is derived from 'Grove's End' from the Old English 'graf' meaning grove and 'ende' meaning end or boundary.

SOUTH BANK OF THE RIVER THAMES

COBHAM
4 miles SE of Gravesend off the A2

This picturesque village is home to one of the largest and finest houses in Kent - **Cobham Hall** - an outstanding red brick mansion that dates from 1584. Set in 150 acres of parkland and demonstrating architectural styles from Elizabethan, Jacobean and Carolean eras and the 18th century, the house has much to offer those interested in art, history and architecture. The Elizabethan wings date from the late 16th century. The central section of the house is later and here can be found the magnificent Gilt Hall that was decorated by Inigo Jones' famous pupil, John Webb, in 1654. Elsewhere in the house there are several superb marble

Cobham Village

fireplaces whilst, outside, lie the beautifully **Gardens** that were landscaped by Humphry Repton for the 4th Earl of Darnley. Over the centuries many notable people have stayed here, including English monarchs from Elizabeth I to Edward VIII, and Charles Dickens used to walk through the grounds from his home at Higham to Cobham's village pub.

Leather Bottle Inn

However, perhaps Cobham Hall's most famous claim to fame dates back to 1883 when Ivo Blight, who later became the 8th Earl of Darnley, led the English cricket team to victory against Australia and brought the Ashes home to Cobham. Today, the hall is a private girls' boarding school and is occasionally open to visitors.

Back in the village more evidence can be found of past members of the Cobham family and, in the 13th century parish church of **St Mary Magdalene**, a series of superb commemorative floor brasses can be seen that date back to the late Middle Ages. Meanwhile, behind the church are some **Almshouses** that incorporate a 14th century kitchen and hall that were once part of the Old College that was founded by the 3rd Lord Cobham. The lord endowed them as living quarters for five priests who were to pray for the repose of his soul and after 1537, when the college was suppressed, the buildings became almshouses.

Finally, in the heart of the village lies the half-timbered **Leather Bottle Inn** that was made famous by Charles Dickens when he featured his favourite inn in the novel *The Pickwick Papers*. It was at the Leather Bottle Inn that Tracey Tupman was discovered by Mr Pickwick after having been jilted by Rachel Wardle.

Close by, just to the north of the village, lies **Owletts** a lovely red brick house that was bought, in the late 17th century, by a Cobham farmer. Still retaining a charming sense of rural comfort the house has an imposing staircase but its main appeal is its modest proportions and beautiful garden.

HEXTABLE
8½ miles SW of Gravesend on the B258

Surrounded by market gardens and orchards, this village is home to **Hextable Gardens**, a heritage centre that lies in the restored Botany Laboratory of Swanley Horticultural College that, itself, is believed to be the first horticultural college in the world. After 1902, Swanley became a horticultural college exclusively for women. Also in the village is **Hextable Park**, a charming place that has been specifically designed to attract a wide variety of wildlife and butterflies. Pictorial information plaques aid visitors in identifying the many species found here.

Chislehurst Pond

CHISLEHURST
13 miles SW of Gravesend on the A208

Following the arrival of the railways, Chislehurst developed as one of London's more select and fashionable suburbs as businessmen took their homes here lured by the mix of fresh air and the hint of the downland scenery that lies on the doorstep. The town has managed to remain a place relatively unspoilt by further development thanks, in large part, to **Chislehurst Common**, an oasis of greenery that is criss-crossed by a number of roads. The suburb is also home to **Chislehurst Caves**, one of Britain's most interesting network of underground caverns. The system of caves, which is entirely man-made, comprises three sections that each relate to a specific era and the oldest section, known as the Druids, dates back approximately 4,000 years. Meanwhile, the largest section is Roman whilst the smallest, and youngest,

Chislehurst Station

HALL PLACE

Bourne Road, Bexley, Kent DA5 1PQ Tel: 01322 526574 Fax: 01322 52292
website: www.hallplaceandgardens.com

Surrounded by its award-winning gardens, **Hall Place** is an attractive mansion house that dates from the 16th century that was substantially added to around 100 years later.

Originally the home of Sir John Champneis, a Lord Mayor of London, the house, over the centuries, has served many purposes and it has been a school on three separate occasions and, during World War II, it was an American Army communications centre.

However, today, parts of the house are open to the public and visitors here can not only see the magnificent Great Hall, the Tudor Parlour and the recently redecorated Drawing Room and Long Gallery but Hall Place contains Bexley Museum and there are also exhibitions galleries. The gardens,

through which the River Cray flows, are impressive and perhaps most eye-catching of all is the outstanding topiary with its chess pieces and Queen's beasts. Meanwhile, there are rose gardens laid out in the Tudor style, herb, rock and heather gardens and a nursery with a display of designs for the smaller garden. Guided tours can be booked of both the house and the gardens. Hall Place is open throughout the year whilst the summer opening Visitors Centre, that doubles as a Tourist Information Centre, hosts exhibitions on local history and arts and crafts.

THE KINGS HEAD

65 High Street, Bexley Village, Bexley, Kent DA5 1AA
Tel: 01322 553137
Fax: 01322 553137

Found in the centre of this historic village, **The Kings Head** is an ancient inn that dates from the 14th century and, along with the pub sign of King Henry VIII, the Cross of St George proudly flies from the building.

An unashamedly traditional inn, stepping inside this listed building is just like going back in time. Copper pots and jugs hang from the old, blackened ceiling beams and there is a large open fireplace whilst pictures of the old village hang from the walls. Warm, friendly and inviting, this is a typical English inn where good food, drink and conversation are the key to the success of the inn. A good selection of real ales, along with lagers, beers and spirits, is available from the bar whilst the menu, backed up by the daily special's board, offers a side choice of traditional English dishes.

Well known and popular thanks to the delicious food and choice of ales, The Kings Head is also a focal point of the village and a busy meeting place that also houses the inn's golf society's trophy cabinet.

was excavated some 1,400 years ago by the Saxons. Royalists took refuge here during the Civil War and the pit that was built to impale their Parliamentarian pursuers can still be seen. More recently, the caves became, at the height of the Blitz during World War II, the world's largest air raid shelter when some 15,000 people hid here from the German bombing raids.

A quiet and pleasant residential area today, Chislehurst has two famous sons: William Willet Junior, the enthusiastic advocate of the Daylight Saving Scheme who unfortunately died a year before British Summer Time (BST) was introduced in 1916; and Sir Malcolm Campbell, the racing driver and pioneering land and water speed record holder of the 1930s.

BEXLEYHEATH
10½ miles W of Gravesend on the A207

Despite being located between Dartford and Woolwich, Bexleyheath is somewhat surprising in that, although there was a great deal of development here in the 19th and early 20th centuries, expanses of parkland still remain. As the town's name might suggest, this area was once heathland and, following enclosure in 1814, some of this land has managed to escape the hands of the developers. In the heart of Bexleyheath lies one of these such areas and **Danson Park** represents an important oasis of greenery.

To the southeast lies **Hall Place** a charming country house that was built in 1540 for Sir John Champneis, a Lord Mayor of London. As well as the fine splendid great hall, the house is particularly noted for its beautiful formal gardens that are laid out on the banks of the River Cray (see panel opposite).

CRAYFORD
8½ miles W of Gravesend on the A2018

Now more a district of the borough of Bexley, it is here that the Roman road, Watling Street, crosses the River Cray. Beside the banks of this river, for over 150 years, the firm David Evans has been printing luxury silks that find their way into High Street shops and fashion houses right around the world. The **World of Silk** provides visitors with an insight into this historic and traditional craft and, on a guided tour, the origins of silk are explained. Believed to have been discovered in around 1640 BC by the Empress of China, Hsi-Ling-Shi, silk found its way to Europe along the arduous silk route and, from the humble silk worm through to the beautiful printed fabrics, the whole of the story of this luxury material is explained. Visitors here will also have the opportunity to visit the factory shop and take refreshment at the coffee shop.

DARTFORD
8 miles W of Gravesend on the A206

This urban settlement is best known as the home of the **Dartford Tunnel** that runs for roughly one mile beneath the River Thames, re-emerging on the Essex bank near West Thurrock. However, Dartford, though not seemingly apparent at first sight, has some historical significance. It stands on the old London to Dover road, at the crossing of the River Darent, and this is the reason for its name which actually means 'Darent Ford'.

It was in Dartford that, in 1381, the **Peasants' Revolt** was sparked off when a tax collector made a personal examination of a young girl to determine whether or not she had reached puberty, when she would have been liable for the unpopular poll tax. Her outraged father, Wat Tyler, killed the tax collector with a hammer and, after being elected their spokesman, led the Kentish peasants on their march to London to demand the abolition of serfdom and relief from their poverty. However, following the fatal stabbing of Tyler by William Walworth, the Lord Mayor of London, at Smithfield in the presence of Richard II, the riot petered out. Although this story is firmly believed by those living in and around Dartford many historians believe that the peasants' leader came from Colchester, in Essex, and that Tyler had not connection with the tax collector's death.

PUDDLEDUCKS

116 St. Johns Hill, Sevenoaks, Kent TN13 3PD
Tel: 01732 743642

Located at the north end of Sevenoaks, on the A225 next to Sevenoaks Hospital, is **Puddleducks**, where visitors can pass through ordinary shop front doors to enter the delightful and colourful world of quilts and wallhangings. The shop sells an array of fabrics, and everything for the patchworker and quilter, all representing excellent value. Here you can stock up on new and unusual fabrics as well as all those little essentials for any keen hobbyist. A small range of hand-made quilted gifts are also on sale, making an ideal gift for yourself, or a friend. Credit cards accepted.

Partners Lesley Porter and Jane O'Neill in addition to running the shop also organise a range of patchwork and quilting courses on the premises, aimed at people of every level of experience and ambition. Courses run from one day to ten weeks in duration, at the end of which time most people are "hooked" on this fulfilling and therapeutic pastime. The courses range from introductory sessions for the novice through to 'troubleshooting' afternoons, courses for specific projects and also sessions for unfinished objects and 'works in progress' - which apparently are very popular! There are also courses in new and unusual techniques and other crafts. Ring for up to date details or a copy of the course list.

THE ROYAL OAK TAP

3 Upper High Street, Sevenoaks,
Kent TN13 1HY
Tel: 01732 458783

Set just south of the main street and, opposite Sevenoaks School and the famous Knole House, is **The Royal Oak Tap**, one of the most animated pubs in the area. The attractions of this free house are its intriguing mix of customers featuring students, sportsmen and foreign visitors to the sights nearby. The pub, which was built in the 16th century, was once a blacksmiths

and is now a listed building. Inside, the "Tap" is open plan, with stone floors, a large inglenook fireplace and old carvings on the bar frontage. As well as substantial lunches there is a good selection of cask ales and wines; manager Julian Mitchell organises barbecues to coincide with satellite TV events. The Royal Oak Tap scores highly, for a town pub, in having its own car park.

SWANSCOMBE
2½ miles W of Gravesend on the A226

This former agricultural village, which has long since been swamped by the growth of industry along the banks of the River Thames, was the site of an important archaeological find in 1935. Excavations in a gravel pit unearthed fragments of a human skull and analysis of the bones revealed that the skull (that of a woman) was around 200,000 years old, making them some of the oldest human remains found in Europe. This riverside settlement also has remnants from more recent historical periods and, while the parish church dates mainly from the 12th century, its structure incorporates bricks from Roman times and parts of its tower predate the Norman invasion. Although the church was substantially restored in the Victorian era, making it difficult to detect the original features, it does provide tangible evidence of the many layers of human settlement here along the Thames.

SEVENOAKS

With its easy road and rail links with London and its leafy and relaxed atmosphere, Sevenoaks has come to epitomise the essence of the commuter belt in many people's eyes. Whilst this perception is not far from the truth, the rural feel of the town was not the creation of garden city planners trying to soften the effect of a large residential and commercial development but it is all that remains of the once wooded countryside that formed the backdrop of the settlement that stood here some nine centuries ago. Sevenoaks began as a market town in Saxon times, although an older settlement is believed to have been sited here previously, and it grew up around the meeting point of the roads from London and the Dartford river crossing as they headed south towards the coast.

The first recorded mention of the town came in 1114, when it was called 'Seovenaca' and local tradition has it that the name refers to the clump of seven oaks that once stood here and, though the trees are now long gone, they were ceremoniously replaced in 1955 with seven trees from Knole Park. These replacement trees made headline news in the autumn of 1987 when several were blown down in the Great Storm that hit the southeast of England in October.

Rural Sevenoaks changed little over the centuries until the arrival of the railway in 1864 and the town became a popular residential area with those working in London. Despite the development, that was again accelerated when the railway line was electrified in the 1930s, Sevenoaks has managed to maintain its

THE VINE TAVERN

11 Pound Lane, Sevenoaks, Kent TN13 3TB
Tel: 01732 741190

The Vine Tavern can be found in the centre of Sevenoaks, just a short stroll from the famous cricket ground. This country hostelry has been given a new lease of life by Dave Robson, who started as manager in 1999. The bar offers at least two real ales, Old Speckled Hen, Greene King and Bass are regularly featured, together with a good range of beer, lager and cider. The food is excellent value for money and served each lunch time, and through the afternoon at weekends. The regular menu offers a good choice of popular dishes while the blackboard offers additional daily specials. In summer, meals and drinks can be enjoyed at the outside tables which overlook a small green.

SNAIL AT STONE STREET

Stone Street,
Seal, Sevenoaks, Kent TN15 0LT
Tel: 01732 810233
Fax: 01732 810020

Found tucked away off the main road between Sevenoaks and Maidstone, the **Snail at Stone Street** is an attractive, old inn that is surrounded by glorious Kent countryside. There is an apple orchard opposite this stone built pub and both Knole Park and Ightham Mote lie close by down these twisting country lanes.

Whilst, outside, the inn has a charming and well established cottage style beer garden, an ideal place to sit in the summer and perfect for children, the interior of this lovely place is intimate and welcoming. A series of small rooms that are each decorated in different styles, there are plenty of cosy corners in which to sit and enjoy a drink from the well stocked bar. Simon Humphries, the experienced manager of the Snail, ensures that everyone receives excellent hospitality from the friendly staff whilst, head chef, Gareth Davies provides a superb menu of tempting dishes. Locally renowned for its cuisine and, in particular, fish the restaurant at the Snail has a bistro atmosphere and the carefully selected wine list provides the perfect accompaniment to any meal here. The restaurant is open from Tuesday to Sunday afternoon and proves so popular that booking at weekends is essential.

THE KENTISH YEOMAN

10-12 High Street, Seal, Sevenoaks, Kent TN15 0AJ
Tel: 01732 761041

In the centre of this small and attractive village, **The Kentish Yeoman** is a friendly public house dating back to the 14th century. This distinctive pub was once the village court and jailhouse. The traditional exterior is of whitewashed stone and tile; it is a large building, taking up much of the road it occupies. A secret tunnel from the cellars to the church still exists, although thankfully the old "hanging tree" has now been cut down. There is an extensive beer garden to the rear and inside, the oak-beamed ceilings and walls add to the characterful ambience. Beers on tap include Courage Best, Marstons Pedigree

and occasional guest ales. There is also a very good choice of wines and spirits. Food is served every day 12.30 -14.30 and Tue-Sat evenings 18.00-20.45; home-cooked and home-prepared, the tempting range of hearty English dishes on offer, including speciality pies, sandwiches and daily specials, is well worth sampling. Duncan and Audrey Lusher are amiable and welcoming hosts, who offer good service and attention to all their guests. Popular with locals and visitors alike, this pub welcomes children and features a changing programme of live entertainment.

individuality and there are still various traditional Kentish tile-hung cottages to be found here. Meanwhile, at the **Sevenoaks Library Gallery** an imaginative programme of contemporary exhibitions of modern art, by both local and international artists, shows that the town does not dwell in the past. Ranging from photography and textiles to fine art, among the various artists featured here have been Andy Warhol and John Piper.

Not far from the centre of Sevenoaks is another reminder of the town's heritage in the form of the **Vine Cricket Ground** that lies on a rise to the south. It was given to the town in 1773 but the first recorded match held here - between Kent and Sussex - was in 1782, when the Duke of Dorset (one of the Sackville family of Knole) and his estate workers defeated a team representing All England. This remarkable victory was particularly sweet as the Duke's team also won a bet of 1,000 guineas!

The pride of Sevenoaks and, for many, of Kent is **Knole House**, one of the largest private homes in England that lies to the southeast of the town and is surrounded by an extensive and majestic deer park.

Bedroom, Knole House

The huge manor house, with its 365 rooms, stands on the site of a much smaller house that was bought by the Archbishop of Canterbury in 1456 and used as an ecclesiastical palace until 1532 when it was taken over by Henry VIII. In 1603, Elizabeth I granted the house to the Sackville family and, although it is now in the ownership of the National Trust, the family still live here. A superb example of late medieval architecture, with Jacobean embellishments that include superb carvings and plasterwork, visitors to Knole can also see the internationally renowned collection of Royal Stuart furnishings that are housed here. An important collection of paintings with works by Van Dyck, Gainsborough, Hoppner and Wootton can be seen too and there are works by Sir Joshua Reynolds which were commissioned for the house by the 3rd Duke of Dorset. Little altered since the 18th century, it was here that Vita Sackville-West was born in 1892 and, as well as

Knole House

THE CROWN

High Street, Otford, Kent
Tel: 01959 522847

Found in the heart of the pleasant and ancient village of Otford, **The Crown** overlooks the historic village pond. Dating back to the 16th century, this typical Kentish building, with its pegtiled roof, makes a colourful addition to this central thoroughfare, especially during the summer months when it is bedecked with flower-filled hanging baskets and window boxes. As traditional an English inn inside as its age suggests, there is a large inglenook fireplace in the bar that, when the log fire is burning during the winter, makes this a warm, cosy and inviting place. As well as the gleaming horse shoe brasses hanging from the ancient ceiling beams, the keen eyed with also spot a selection of large keys and foreign bank notes.

However, whilst the surroundings here are certainly attractive The Crown, under the management of local man, Matthew Lake, also offers its customers superb hospitality. A selection of real ales, along with all the usual drinks, are available from the bar and there is food here throughout the week - except Sunday evening. The traditional menu, that also includes such favourites as curries, is sure to please everyone but it is worth remembering that Friday evening is fish night - fresh from Rye - and the choice of three roasts on Sunday lunchtimes are particularly popular.

FORGE HOUSE RESTAURANT

30 High Street, Otford, Sevenoaks, Kent TN14 5PQ
Tel: 01959 522463 Fax: 01959 522463 website: www.forgehouse.co.uk

Dating back to the 16th century the building that houses **Forge House Restaurant** is a particularly impressive example of typical Kentish architecture. Originally a row of dwellings, this superb building, with its peg tile roof and small leaded cottage windows, has certainly withstood the test of time. First impressions of the restaurant are completed by the colourful array of flowering plants, shrubs and creepers that adorn the front of the restaurant. Despite appearing to be a large restaurant from the outside, the interior has been divided by an ornamental pond that not only makes an interesting feature but that also, along with the heavily beamed ceiling, creates a cosy and intimate atmosphere.

Forge House has been owned and personally run by Shukri Harper since 1989 and, although Shukri comes from Cyprus, the menu is predominantly French with a traditional English menu for Sunday lunch. Dishes range from popular winter favourites such as Steak and kidney pie to Scotch lobster and calves liver and it is not surprising that, with a carefully choice wine list to match, the Forge House Restaurant has a loyal following of discerning customers. Naturally, as this is a popular restaurant, booking is essential.

being the setting for Virgina Wolff's novel *Orlando*, it is believed that Hitler intended to use Knole as his English headquarters.

GATEWAY TO KENT

OTFORD
3 miles N of Sevenoaks off the A225

Found in a pleasant location beside the River Darent, this village has a history that stretches back to Roman times and beyond - as does much of the Darent Valley. Lying at an important crossroads for many centuries, it was here, in AD 775, that King Offa of Mercia fought against the men of Kent and, several hundred years later, Henry VIII stopped at Otford on his way to the historic encounter with Francois I of France at the Field of the Cloth of Gold. The King is believed to have stayed the night at one of the many palaces belonging to the Archbishop of Canterbury and the palace at Otford, of which little of the original building now remains, stood adjacent to the Church of St Bartholomew and opposite the village's duck pond.

The **Pond**, which lies at the heart of Otford, is itself something of an historic curio as it was documented as early as the 11th century and it is thought to be the only stretch of water in England to be classified as a listed building. The **Otford Heritage Centre** is just the place to find out more about this interesting village and here can be seen displays on the village's natural history, geology and archaeology, including artefacts from nearby Roman sites and the medieval Archbishop's Palace.

Connections with the Archbishops of Canterbury continue at **Becket's Well** that once supplied water to the palace and that is thought to have miraculous

THE WOODMAN

2 High Street, Otford, Sevenoaks, Kent TN14 5PQ
Tel: 01959 522195

In the small town of Otford, just a couple of miles north of Sevenoaks, visitors will find **The Woodman** located on the main street near to the village green. The pub dates back to the 18th century when it was built as a wheelwright's business. There is reputed to be a tunnel which leads from under the pub to the castle though it has never been found. Like many old buildings, there is also a resident ghost which has been seen by a number of customers over the years.

Behind the imposing frontage you will find a large interior with comfortable bar areas offering plenty of seating. On tap are usually kept two or three real ales, with Masterbrew and Spitfire always available, together with a good range of draught

lager. An excellent range of food is served daily with the lunch and evening menus offering a good variety of dishes to suit all tastes. A new restaurant area is planned and will be constructed to the rear of the present property offering improved facilities and more seating - due to open Summer 2002.

The Woodman offers a programme of regular live music acts on Friday and Saturday nights and Sunday lunch - ring for details. Rates are very reasonable, with Low Season and Winter savers, group discounts and special Christmas and New Year packages.

STAR HOUSE

Star Hill, Sevenoaks, Kent TN14 6HA
Tel: 01959 533109

Although **Star House** lies close to the M25 and within easy reach of London, Maidstone and Brands Hatch, the immediate surroundings would suggest that the house is miles from anywhere. A family home for over 50 years, owners, Anne and Keith Viner offer superb bed and breakfast accommodation that must be hard to better.

This large and spacious Victorian house was built on the site of an ancient pub and is, today, surrounded by a massive seven acre garden. Here, there is a heated outdoor swimming pool for guests to use in the summer, whilst, the grounds also feature an extensive water garden that was created in an old chalk quarry and that still contains the old kiln. As the grounds slope away from the house, there are wonderful panoramic views over the Darent Valley and beyond to the North Downs.

The accommodation here comprises three generously sized guest rooms - a family room, twin room and a double - and each has been tastefully decorated and furnished with guests' comfort in mind. Those staying here can also relax in front of the open fire in the guest lounge and, for breakfast, those staying here all meet around the refectory table in the dining room for breakfast where, again, there are magnificent views from the windows.

THE RISING SUN

Cotmans Ash Lane, Woodlands,
near Kemsing, Sevenoaks,
Kent TN15 6XD
Tel: 01959 522683

Found in the heart of this rural hamlet, that is also home to the renowned Woodlands Golf Club, **The Rising Sun** is a lovely country inn that is well worth taking the trouble to find. Thought to be over 400 years old, this beautiful, traditional Kentish building, of flint and bricks with a peg tiled roof, remains fabulously unspoilt and unchanged by the modern age. The inn is owned and personally run by Michelle and

Peter Hunter, who first found it as customers and they certainly know what their own customers enjoy. Helped by their son Ben and daughter Kelly, this lovely inn is just the place to experience the very best in hospitality in a very English pub setting.

Michelle breeds Dexter cattle and it is their beef that appears on the superb inn menu. Peter and Ben are the chefs and, along with the traditional pub fayre, they include plenty of game when in season as well as locally caught fish. The range and extent of the drinks from the bar matches the imagination and high standards of the food here and nobody coming here will be surprised to find that The Rising Sun appears in the CAMRA Good Beer Guide.

origins. Local folklore suggests that when he was visiting Otford, Archbishop Thomas à Becket was so displeased with the quality of the local water that, to remedy the situation, he struck the ground with his crozier and two springs of clear water bubbled up from the spot.

SHOREHAM
4 miles N of Sevenoaks off the A255

Riverside, Shoreham

Shoreham is situated beside the River Darent, which features prominently in the village. As well as the footpaths that run along its banks, it is also crossed by a handsome hump-backed bridge. Close to this bridge lies the **Water House** that was the home of Samuel Palmer for some years and from where Palmer entertained his friend the poet and visionary William Blake.

On the hillside across the valley can be seen a large cross carved into the chalk that commemorates those who died in the two World Wars. Meanwhile, **Shoreham**

CHURCH HOUSE

Church Street, Shoreham,
near Sevenoaks, Kent TN14 7SB
Tel: 01959 522241 Fax: 01959 522241
e-mail: katehowie@compuserve.com

Standing in more than three acres of lovely gardens and shielded from the village lane by a hefty yew hedge, **Church House** is a restful and tranquil bed and breakfast establishment. The house itself is Georgian, dating from around 1750, although the frontage - first seen when entering through the graceful yew archway - is Victorian. The three guest rooms, one of which is en suite, are spacious and handsomely

decorated. There are lovely views out over the grounds and surrounding countryside. Downstairs there is a private drawing room for guests that is decorated with several Georgian touches.

Kate Howie, the owner of Church House, can trace the Howie name back to the 12th century. She is good company and enjoys talking about history with guests. Much of this history has a decided gardening slant to it- not surprising since Kate has a diploma in the History, Design and Maintenance of Gardens in addition to her qualifications in hotel and catering management. The extensive gardens, which are at the guests' disposal, feature ponds, an interesting gazebo and an all-weather tennis court whilst the recently renovated front garden now has a box parterre depicting Kate's initials that is particularly in keeping with the age of the house. A short walk takes visitors to the four local pubs and the local rail station with its quick connections to London.

Brands Hatch

Aircraft Museum is dedicated to the Battle of Britain and the air war over southern England. Among the numerous exhibits are aviation relics and homefront memorabilia from the 1940s and, as well as learning more about the brave pilots who defended the country from invasion, visitors can also view the aviation paintings and prints that are for sale and enjoy tea and home-made cakes in the café.

EYNSFORD
6½ miles N of Sevenoaks off the A225

The centre of this pretty and picturesque village manages to preserve a sense of history and, crossing the River Darent, there is a small hump-backed bridge and an ancient ford along with a number of old timbered cottages and a church with a tall shingle spire. Though the ford, which gives the village its name, is still passable by cars there is a depth chart beside it that shows that the depth of the ford can reach six feet when the river is swollen with floodwater. The village has certainly had its fair share of famous inhabitants and, in particular, it was the home of Pater Warlock, the pseudonym of Philip Heseltine, who composed over 100 songs, many of which had a rural theme. Leslie

Hore-Belisha also made his home here for a time and, if his name sounds familiar, it was whilst Minister of Transport in the 1930s that Leslie gave his name to the Belisha beacon street crossings and he also inaugurated the driving test for motorists.

Just a short distance from the village, and found down a lane, is **Eagle Heights**, Kent's bird of prey centre that was established to further the cause of British birds. Concentrating on explaining the importance of conservation and the birds' environment, the centre hosts free flying shows where visitors can see eagles soaring high above the Darent Valley and watch the Condor, the world's largest bird of prey, fly. Meanwhile there are indoor demonstrations, when snakes can be handled, and other attractions that will delight the whole family.

Further down the lane lies **Lullingstone Roman Villa** that was only uncovered in 1949 although its existence had been known since the 18th century when farm labourers uncovered fragments of mosaics that had been pierced as the men drove fence posts into the ground. Although not the largest find in the country, Lullingstone is recognised to be the most exciting of its kind made in the 20th century and, along with the splendid mosaic floors, the villa, which was first occupied in AD 80, is home to one of the earliest private Christian chapels.

Close by lies **Lullingstone Castle**, a superb manor house whose 15th century gatehouse is one of the first ever to be built from bricks. The house has some fine state rooms, as might be expected of a place that had associations with both

Henry VIII and Queen Anne, as well as family portraits and amour on display. The castle is surrounded by beautiful grounds that also house the Norman church of St Botolph. A little further south again lies **Lullingstone Park and Visitor Centre** that incorporates both parkland, with ancient pollared oaks, and chalk grassland. A full programme of guided

Riverside, Farningham

walks, special events and children's activities take place from the visitor centre where there is a countryside interpretation exhibition.

FARNINGHAM
8 miles N of Sevenoaks off the A225

This attractive village, in the Darent valley, was once on the main London road and much of the Georgian architecture found in the village centre reflects the prosperity that Farningham once enjoyed. A handsome 18th century brick bridge stands by lawns that slope down to the river's edge, alongside which runs the

Darent Valley Path, that follows the course of the river as far as Dartford. Despite its rural appeal, Farningham is close to the M25 and M20 motorway intersection, but **Farningham Woods Nature Reserve** provides a delightful area of natural countryside that supports a wide variety of rare plants and birdlife.

MEOPHAM
10 miles NE of Sevenoaks on the A227

This pretty village, whose name is pronounced 'Meppam', still acts as a trading centre for the surrounding smaller villages and hamlets. As well as the well maintained cricket green, the village is home to **Meopham Windmill**, a fully restored black smock mill dating from 1821 that is unusual in that it has six sides. The village was the birthplace of the great 17th century naturalist and gardener John Tradescant, who introduced many non-native species of flowers and vegetables into England.

Farningham Centre

DUKE OF WELLINGTON

The Street, Ryarsh, near West Malling, Kent ME19 5LS
Tel: 01732 842318

Situated on the main road through this village, the **Duke of Wellington** is a large and distinguished inn that has a long history. Originally built in 1515, during the reign of Henry VIII, the inn stands on the site of a refectory and chapel that can be traced back to the time of the Norman Conquest and that also featured in the Domesday Book. Owned by Benedictine monks, they began distributing their own home brew and, in 1516, the Duke of Wellington was granted a license to sell just ales and ciders. Over 100 years later, in the 1640s, the inn underwent extensive alterations that included the removal of the building's thatch and the replacement of much of the wattle and daub although a portion has been preserved and can be seen inside. Finally, the inn took its present name to honour the Duke's great victory over Napoleon in June 1815.

Today, the inn remains an interesting blend of ancient and more modern and the interior is unashamedly traditional old English in style. The wooden floor extends throughout the various rooms of this inn and customers have the choice of the cosy snug, sitting in front of the large inglenook fireplace in the main bar or eating in the wood panelled dining room.

Vince and Kathy Galloway, first made their acquaintance with the Duke of Wellington when they came here as managers and, since 1997, they have been the friendly and hospitable owners. Kathy is

a local lady, whilst Vince, from Ireland, trained as a chef and his background is evident in the extremely good food served here. A traditional pub menu is served at lunchtime with favourites such as steak and kidney pies and ploughman's lunches but, in the evening, the selection changes to an interesting and surprising mix of dishes from around the world. Well known for its moules mariniere and with ale featuring in many of the dishes, the Duke of Wellington comes very highly recommended. Likewise, Vince is equally proud of his cellar and, along with the usual drinks, there is always a real Kentish ale. With popular live traditional jazz evenings every Thursday and a petanque piste outside in the beer garden, this is an inn that caters for everyone.

TROTTISCLIFFE
9½ miles NE of Sevenoaks off the A20

As its name implies, this village occupies a hillside position but those visiting Trottiscliffe should take note as its name is actually pronounced 'Trosley'! A pretty, neat village with views over the North Downs, it was the beauty of this quiet place that lured the artist Graham Sutherland to make Trottiscliffe his home.

Just to the north of the village, on high ground that offers commanding views eastwards over the Medway Valley, stands **Coldrum Long Barrow**, some 24 columns of stone that once marked the perimeter of a circular long barrow that was originally 50 feet in diameter. Only four of the huge stones are still standing and, although the huge burial mound inside the circle has long since disappeared, this ancient site remains an evocative and mysterious place.

WROTHAM
6 miles NE of Sevenoaks off the A227

This ancient village, whose name is pronounced 'Rootum', was once a staging post on one of the important routes southeastwards from London. It was here, in 1536, that Henry VIII received news of the execution of his second wife, Anne Boleyn.

PLATT
6 miles E of Sevenoaks off the A25

This village lies close to **Great Comp Garden**, one of finest gardens in the country and one that has a truly unique atmosphere. Along with the ruins of the house that once stood surrounded by the grounds, there are terraces and sweeping lawn along with a breathtaking collection of trees, shrubs and perennials and, by contrast, tranquil woodland walks.

THRIFTWOOD CARAVAN AND CAMPING PARK

Wrotham Hill, Plaxdale Green Road, Stansted,
nr Wrotham, Kent TN15 7PB
Tel: 01732 822261 Fax: 01732 824636
website: www.ukparks.co.uk/thriftwood

Thriftwood Caravan and Camping Park has built up a loyal and appreciative following. Owners Geoffrey and Evelyn Bass have run this superb park for six years, and the site makes good use of its scenic position. On the edge of this quiet village, there are lovely walks in the area, including The Pilgrims' Way and the North Downs Way, and it is only 35 minutes by train from London's Victoria station. This sheltered site can accommodate 150 touring vans and 20 static holiday homes. Electric hookups are available, as well as modern toilets, heated showers, public telephone, launderette, ice-pack freezer and cooking facilities. The site boasts many delightful features, such as a swimming pool, children's safe play area.

This award-winning caravan park has approximately 12 acres of camping area. The surroundings offer a wealth of natural beauty, including flowers, shrubs, trees and native wildlife. This picturesque

park is an ideal base for exploring London (the site is just 35 minutes by train to Victoria Station), Kent's stately homes, castles, beautiful gardens, countryside and the surrounding regions, and is only 30 minutes from the Channel. The site also includes a fine tourist information centre, well-stocked shop and small bar, offering a wide range of beers, wines and spirits, tea and fresh coffee. Visitors are assured of a warm, traditional English welcome. Local sporting facilities include golfing, tennis, fishing and motor racing (at Brands Hatch). Superb six-berth and beautifully equipped holiday homes are available for hire. Open March - January.

IGHTHAM
4½ miles E of Sevenoaks on the A227

This delightful village, whose name is pronounced 'Item', is a charming place of half-timbered houses and crooked lanes and visitors coming here to visit Ightham Mote, which lies further south at Ivy Hatch, should certainly not rush away. Inside **Ightham church** is a mural dedicated to Dame Dorothy Selby who, according to legend, was instrumental in uncovering the Gunpowder Plot. The story goes that James I showed Dame Dorothy an anonymous letter he had received that hinted at 'a terrible blow' that would soon befall Parliament and, whilst the king dismissed the letter as the work of a crank, Dame Dorothy, understanding the implications, urged him to take the warning with the utmost seriousness.

IVY HATCH
3½ miles E of Sevenoaks off the A227

Just to the south of this small village lies **Ightham Mote**, one of England's finest medieval manor houses that is owned by the National Trust. Covering some 650 years of history, this beautiful moated house, set in a narrow, wooded valley, dates back to the 14th century. It is constructed around a central courtyard that retains the meeting place purpose that is referred to in its name - 'mote' probably comes from the Old English word meaning 'meeting place'. There is plenty to see here, from the medieval Great Hall and Tudor chapel to the Victorian housekeeper's room and the billiard room. There is also an exhibition that details the traditional skills that were used during the major conservation programme which took place here in 1998. Meanwhile, the delightful garden

ROSE AND CROWN

High Street, Wrotham, near Sevenoaks,
Kent TN15 7AE
Tel: 01732 882409

Dating back to around the mid 18th century, the **Rose and Crown** is a large inn that lies in the heart of this small town. Although it stands right on the main street, there is, to the rear, a patio style beer garden and, in the summer, the hanging baskets here are so impressive that they have won various local awards. Inside, the interior is not only spacious, with a central bar, but has a true traditional atmosphere that is created by the polished wood floor and

the wood burning stove and open fireplace. There is also rumoured to be a resident ghost who possibly has a dislike for windmills as two of the paintings, of windmills, have mysteriously fallen from different walls without their strings breaking! Other paintings on the walls (most of which are for sale) are by local artists and some by landlady, Julie. Along with her husband, Alan, the couple have been here since 1995 and, in that time, they have certainly put the inn on the local map. The excellent condition of the real ales served here earned the pub a mention in the Good Beer Guide whilst the home-made food makes this a popular place for a meal. The menu changes regularly and, along with the hearty soups and tasty pies, the Wrotham Hotpot - made with lamb - is something of a speciality here. The headquarters of the Hartley Morris Dancers and a regular meeting place for other local societies and groups, this friendly inn does much work for charity and, visitors will be interested to learn, also offers bed and breakfast accommodation.

Ightham Mote

rise up from the orchards and, at the top, is one of southern England's largest forests, **Mereworth Woods**. Wild boar once roamed through this forest of oak and beech trees and, though today the wildlife is of a tamer variety, the woods are still enchanting.

MEREWORTH
8 miles E of Sevenoaks on the A228

Found on the southern boundary of Mereworth Woods, the village is something of a curiosity. Early in the 18th century, John Fane, a local landowner, built himself a large Palladian mansion here. However, he soon became disappointed as the village obscured some of his views of the surrounding countryside and so he had the village demolished and moved to a site that could not be seen from his new home. The new village had houses for all the original inhabitants and Fane even built a new church. This being the 1740s, the church architecture owes a lot to the style of Sir Christopher Wren and the result is a faithful copy of St Martin in the Fields, London.

BIGGIN HILL
7½ miles NW of Sevenoaks on the A233

This village is best known for its association with the RAF and, in particular, with the role that the local station played in the Battle of Britain. A Spitfire and a Hurricane flank the entrance to **Biggin Hill RAF Station** and they are silent reminders of the stalwart service of these two aircraft, and their crews, during the dark days of World War II. A chapel at the station commemorates

and grounds, with their lakes and woodland, provide numerous opportunities for pleasant country walks.

PLAXTOL
4½ miles E of Sevenoaks off the A227

This hilltop village, on a prominent ridge near Ightham Mote, has a charming row of traditional Kentish weatherboard cottages that surround the parish church. Just to the east of the village, and reached via a circuitous succession of narrow lanes, is **Old Soar Manor**, another fine National Trust owned manor house that dates from the late 13th century. Originally built as a knight's dwelling, the house seen today occupies the solar block and of particular interest here are the undercrofts with their graceful vaults curving upwards. Whilst the house itself is charming it is the idyllic setting of Old Soar Manor, with its surrounding orchards and copses, that makes this such a delightful place to visit. The woods grow more dense as they climb the ridge and

HIGH ELMS COUNTRY PARK

Shire Lane, Farnborough, Kent BR6 7JH
Tel: 01689 862815 Fax: 01689 861347

Found on the rim of the River Thames basin, on a ridge of the North Downs, **High Elms Country Park** is a wonderful expanse of woodland, formal gardens and wildflower meadows yet it is only 15 miles from central London. Covering some 250 acres, the peaceful country park trails, that have been created to highlight various aspects of the park for visitors, tell little of the park's eventful history.

Originally, along with adjacent golf course, this park formed the estate of High Elms that, in the early 19th century came into the hands of the Lubbock family. For the next 130 years or so the family farmed and expanded the estate and it was the 3rd Baronet, in the Victorian era, who commissioned the building of the grand mansion house along with the ornate Italian gardens. A race course too was built and the last race meeting held on the estate was attended by some 40,000 people.

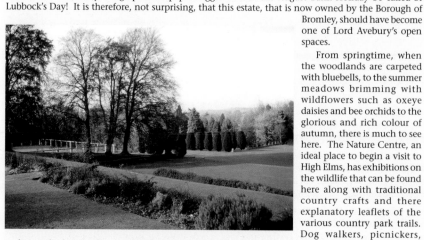

Whilst, the 3rd Baronet was certainly flamboyant it was his successor, who was given the title of Lord Avebury in 1900, who is best remembered. A banker, politician, author and scientist, Sir John Lubbock was instrumental in introducing 30 Acts of Parliament including The Open Spaces Act and The Wild Birds Protection Act. However, it was for the introduction of Bank Holidays that made Lord Avebury famous, so much so, in fact, that the Daily Telegraph newspaper suggested that the August Bank Holiday be called St Lubbock's Day! It is therefore, not surprising, that this estate, that is now owned by the Borough of Bromley, should have become one of Lord Avebury's open spaces.

From springtime, when the woodlands are carpeted with bluebells, to the summer meadows brimming with wildflowers such as oxeye daisies and bee orchids to the glorious and rich colour of autumn, there is much to see here. The Nature Centre, an ideal place to begin a visit to High Elms, has exhibitions on the wildlife that can be found here along with traditional country crafts and there explanatory leaflets of the various country park trails. Dog walkers, picnickers, cyclists and riders are all catered for here and, whilst the park is certainly popular, there is ample space to find a quiet and peaceful corner. A Site of Special Scientific Interest and one that also hosts a number of annual events for all the family, the combination of managed conservation and informal leisure works harmoniously to provide a wonderful and interesting day out for everyone.

the 453 pilots from Biggin Hill who lost their lives during the conflict. The location of Biggin Hill - high on a plateau on the North Downs - made it an obvious choice for an airfield and the views from here, over the Darent Valley, are outstanding.

Meanwhile, the village itself, which sprawls along this plateau, has a particularly interesting church that was built almost single-handedly by the local vicar, between 1955 and 1959, using material from the derelict All Saints' Church at Peckham.

DOWNE
7 miles NW of Sevenoaks off the A233

Found high up on the North Downs and commanding spectacular views, especially northwards towards London, Downe has managed to retain a real country atmosphere and its central core of traditional flint cottages has not been engulfed by the growing tide of modern suburban housing spreading from the capital. Seemingly at a crossroads between Greater London and the countryside, Downe's natural setting, still evident in the outskirts of the village, also marks something of a boundary as it is poised between the open uplands of the Downs themselves and the more wooded areas of Kent, such as the Weald, further south.

It was in this village, at **Down House**, that one of the world's greatest and best known scientists, Charles Darwin, lived for over 40 years until his death in 1882. Following his five year voyage on *HMS Beagle*, Darwin came back to this house where he worked on formalising his theory of evolution and it was here that he wrote his famous work *The Origin of Species by Means of Natural Selection* that was published in 1859. The house is now a museum dedicated to the life and work

of this famous scientist and visitors can not only find out more about his revolutionary theory but also gain an understanding of the man himself. The study, where he did much of his writing, still contains many personal belongings and the family rooms too have been painstakingly restored to provide a real insight into Charles Darwin, the scientist, husband and father.

FARNBOROUGH
8 miles NW of Sevenoaks off the A223

Just to the south of the village lies **High Elms Country Park**, a delightful park of woodlands, formal gardens and meadows, that was once part of the High Elms Estate (see panel opposite).

ORPINGTON
8 miles NW of Sevenoaks on the A232

Once a country village, between the two World Wars, Orpington changed dramatically into the commuter town that it is today. However, thanks to William Cook, a 19th century local poultry farmer, the town has not lost its rural connections as Cook introduced a breed of poultry - the Black Orpington - that was to become famous throughout the farming world in Britain, Europe and beyond. In the heart of the town, next to the library, stands **Bromley Museum** that is an ideal place from which to begin an exploration of this area. With plenty to see, from prehistoric relics right through to the lives of Bromley people in the 20th century, visitors should not overlook this lovely medieval building and the pleasant surrounding gardens (see panel on page 24).

Close to the town centre, and protected from the elements by a modern cover building, is **Crofton Roman Villa** that was built in around AD 140 and inhabited for over 250 years. Presumed to have

BROMLEY MUSEUM

The Priory, Church Hill, Orpington, Kent BR6 0HH
Tel: 01689 873826

Housed in a museum piece itself, an interesting medieval building dating from 1290, and surrounded by attractive gardens **Bromley Museum** has numerous exhibits and displays that cover the history of the area around Bromley. From prehistoric Stone Age tools, Roman lamps and Saxon jewellery to a recreated 1930s dining room and memorabilia from World War II there are many interesting items that will fire the imagination. The museum is also home an archaeological collection that was put together by Victorian 'Renaissance man' Sir John Lubbock of nearby Hall Place (see panel on page 6).

been at the centre of a farming estate, the villa, which was altered several times during its occupation, probably extended to some 20 rooms although the remains of only 10 have been uncovered. Evidence of the under-floor heating arrangements, or hypocaust, can still be seen as can some of the tiled floors and there is a display of the artefacts that were also uncovered during the excavations here.

TONBRIDGE

This pretty old town stands at the highest navigable point on the River Medway and, as well as having a Victorian cast iron bridge across the river, the substantial remains of Tonbridge's Norman **Castle** can be found on a rise in the town centre. The walls of the castle date from the 12th century while the shell of the keep, along with the massive gatehouse and drum towers, were built in the early 14th century. Within the castle walls is a mound that is believed to have been the site of an earlier Saxon fort that provides further evidence of the importance that the river crossing here once had. The castle was all but destroyed during the Civil War and, today, the ruins are surrounded by landscaped gardens.

Whilst the castle is certainly one of the town's oldest buildings, its most famous

institution is **Tonbridge School** that was founded in 1553 by Sir Andrew Judd, Master of the Skinners' Company and a former Lord Mayor of London. The school received a charter from Elizabeth I and, on Judd's death, the administration was left in trust to the Skinners' Company which remain the Governors to this day. The school is mainly housed in 19th century buildings on the High Street, where other attractive 18th and 19th century buildings can also be found.

THE SURREY BORDERS

PENSHURST
4½ miles SW of Tonbridge on the B2176

With its hilly, wooded setting and Tudor architecture, Penshurst is renowned as being one of Kent's prettiest villages. The houses at its core are all old, dating from 200 to 500 years ago, and each has its own sense of charm and identity. At the heart of the village is the 12th century Church of St John the Baptist that, as well as containing architectural details from the 13th, 14th and 15th centuries, is also reached by an ancient lych-gate. Close by is one of the village's equally ancient houses, a two storey Tudor dwelling that is particularly quaint with its bulging walls and crooked beams.

Just to the north of the village lies

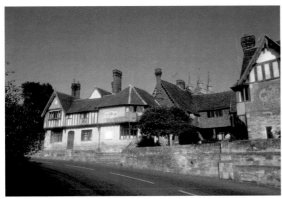

Penshurst Village

Penshurst Place, one of England's finest historic houses and a wonderful example of 14th century architecture. Originally built in 1341, the house was given to Sir William Sidney in the mid 16th century by Edward VI and the family have continued to live here ever since. This imposing fortified manor house is surrounded by beautiful and peaceful **Gardens** that are a rare survivor of the Elizabethan age and that provide colour throughout the year. Penshurst Place is also home to a **Toy Museum**, whilst, for the more energetic, there are also nature trails and a children's venture playground along with a restaurant, gift shop and plant centre (see panel below).

Also close by is one of the most modern vineyards in England, **Penshurst Vineyard**, where adults can enjoy the lovely walks and the wine tastings and children can watch the unusual range of

PENSHURST PLACE AND GARDENS

Penshurst, Tonbridge, Kent TN11 8DG
Tel: 01892 870307 Fax: 08192 870866
e-mail: enquiries@penshurstplace.com
website: www.penshurstplace.com

Set in the peaceful landscape of the Weald of Kent, Penshurst Place is recognised as being one of the best examples of 14th century architecture in the country. The house was built of local sandstone in 1341 and, in 1552, Edward VI granted Penshurst Place to his steward and tutor, Sir William Sidney, grandfather of the famous Elizabethan poet, soldier and courtier, Sir Philip Sidney. Additions to the

original house, over the centuries, have seen it become an imposing fortified manor house and it remains in the Sidney family today. Visitors here have the opportunity not only to see the magnificent Barons Hall and the impressive staterooms but also a marvellous collection of paintings, furniture, tapestries, porcelain and armour.

Meanwhile, the Gardens surrounding the house are equally impressive and are a rare example of Elizabethan design. The records here go back to 1346, making this one of the oldest gardens in private ownership, and over a mile of yew hedging separates the walled garden into a series of individually styled 'rooms'. Designed as a garden for all seasons, visitors here can enjoy a riot of colour from early spring right through to the autumn.

Penshurst Place is also the home of a Toy Museum, where the world of the nursery is brought to life through an interesting collection of dolls, tin soldiers and many other toys that originally belonged to several generations of the Sidney children.

PENSHURST VINEYARDS

Grove Road, Penshurst, Tonbridge,
Kent TN11 8DU
Tel: 01892 870255 Fax: 01892 870255
website www.penshurst.co.uk

Penshurst Vineyards welcomes visitors to a vineyard with a difference. Not only are you offered an insight into the production of high quality wines, but you can also enjoy a unique collection of wildlife - a delightful combination that attracts thousands of visitors each year. The picturesque location just outside the village of Penshurst, close to the Eden Valley, makes this an ideal family day out.

The first planting was of just three acres on a south facing slope in the spring of 1972 and by 1975 the first grapes were harvested resulting in a high quality wine that was enjoyable to drink. Following a bumper harvest in 1976 additional varieties were planted and by 1979 the vineyard reached its present size of 12 acres. The modern winery that visitors see today was built in 1981 and since then all the wine has been produced on site, going on to win many medals and awards. Guided tours can be arranged by appointment and include an insight into growing grapes, the equipment used in the production of high quality wines, a free tasting and a talk on wine appreciation. The centre-piece of the winery is the 4,000 litre wooden cask which has a reproduction of the Penshurst wine label carved into it.

The wildlife collection includes a mob of wallabies which, with the black swans and flock of rare breed sheep, are a great attraction. The wallabies, which are bred here, feature strongly in the history of Penshurst Vineyard, with a picture of one being incorporated into the wine label! The estate has also become a breeding centre for more than 30 species of exotic wildfowl.

THE GREYHOUND

Charcott,
near Chiddingstone Causeway,
Kent TN11 8LG
Tel: 01892 870275

Found in the centre of the tucked away hamlet of Charcott and yet close to local attractions such as Hever Castle and Chartwell, **The Greyhound** is a true hidden place that is well worth seeking out. Built at the end of the 19th century, this attractive pub has a patio area to the front, that is decorated with hanging baskets and flower-filled troughs, whilst, to the side and the rear of the building there is a large, lawned beer garden.

Well known as purveyors of fine cask ales, wines, spirits and the most wholesome of victuals, hosts Mary and Arthur Tabrett also offer their customers a charming and traditional environment in which to enjoy the friendly hospitality here. They came to The Greyhound in 1992, after some years living and farming in Tenerife, and since then have established a large and loyal local following. A fine selection of drinks, including real ales, can be found at the bar, where there are open fires in winter and hop bines hanging from the ceiling. Mary is the chef of the partnership and the tasty menu that is offered here every day but Tuesdays provides a wide selection of tempting home-made dishes. Whilst Mary is locally famous for her Sunday roast lunches, during the winter, there is a regular steak and kidney pudding club which is not only very popular but also draws people from a large area. A warm and friendly pub where both locals and visitors are welcomed with open arms.

Penshurst Place

houses Bower's vast ranging collection that covers such far reaching themes as relics from ancient Egypt and artefacts from Japan to pictures and mementoes from the Royal Stuart dynasty.

BOUGH BEECH
6½ miles W of Tonbridge on the B2027

To the north of this village lies **Bough Beech Reservoir** whose surrounding nature reserve provides excellent opportunities for bird watching. Meanwhile, the reservoir's visitor centre has a series of exhibitions and displays on the local wildlife, the area's hop growing industry and the history of this reservoir.

animals, including wallabies, rare breeds of sheep and birds, that have their home here (see panel opposite).

CHIDDINGSTONE
6 miles W of Tonbridge off the B2027

This pretty village, set in pleasant open woodland, is one of the most picturesque in Kent and it is owned by the National Trust. Along a footpath behind the main street, which is lined with houses from the 16th and 17th centuries that were built during the village's prosperous period, lies a block of sandstone known as the **Chiding Stone**. Legend has it that in the past miscreant, vagrants and assorted petty criminals were taken here for public humiliation

Also found in this village is one of Kent's best kept secrets, **Chiddingstone Castle**, a traditional country squire's house that has the appearance of a grand castle. A reworking of a much older house and the home of the Streatfeild family, in 1955 the house was bought by connoisseur Denys Eyre Bower, a self-made man whose particular passion was collecting. Today, the castle

HEVER
7½ miles W of Tonbridge off the B2027

This tiny village, set in a delightfully unspoilt countryside of orchards and woodlands, is home to one of Kent's star attractions - **Hever Castle**. The original castle, that consisted of the gatehouse, outer walls and inner moat, was built in

Hever Castle

The Drawbridge, Hever Castle

the 1270s by Sir Stephen de Penchester who received permission from Edward I to greatly fortify his home. Some two centuries later, the Bullen (or Boleyn) family purchased the property and they added the comfortable Tudor manor house that stands within the castle walls.

Hever Castle was the childhood home of Anne Boleyn and the ill-fated mother of Elizabeth I was courted here by Henry VIII. Many of Anne's personal items, including two books of hours (prayer books) signed by Anne, along with other Tudor mementoes can be seen here.

In 1903, the castle was bought by the American millionaire, William Waldorf Astor and he used his great wealth to restore the original buildings and the grounds - work that included laying out and planting over 30 acres of formal gardens. These award winning gardens are certainly one of the main features here to which visitors are drawn but the castle also houses fine collections of paintings, furniture, tapestries and objects d'art

EDENBRIDGE
9 miles W of Tonbridge on the B2026

This small town, found near the upper reaches of the River Eden, has been a settlement since Roman times and, although the present bridge spanning the river dates from the 1830s, there has been a bridge here since that early occupation. The Roman road that crossed the river was an important route through the forest of the Kentish Weald and along its route can still be found ancient coaching inns, some dating from as long ago as the 1370s, that catered to the needs of travellers.

The town's name seems to be simply explained since there is a bridge here and it passes over the River Eden. However, the bridge is actually named after a Saxon leader, Eadhelm, whose river crossing replaced the earlier Roman structure. The name of the town settled easily into Edenbridge and the river, that was without a name in Saxon times, became known as the Eden.

The Maze, Hever Castle

IDE HILL
7½ miles NW of Tonbridge off the B2042

Situated in the upper Darent Valley, this small village provides, from its elevated position, glorious, panoramic views stretching out over the Weald. Just outside the village, and set on a hillside of mature beech trees, is **Emmetts Garden** an informal National Trust maintained garden that boasts the highest tree top in Kent - a 100 foot Wellingonia planted on the Kent's highest point (some 700 feet above sea level). Noted for its rare trees and shrubs, as well as its rose and rock gardens, Emmetts also offers wonderful views across the Kentish Weald.

FRENCH STREET
8½ miles NW of Tonbridge off the B2042

A tiny hamlet, tucked away in the folds of narrow, wooded hills, French Street appears to be one of the most hidden away places in Kent. In fact, if it is was not for the famous house that lies close by, it is probable that few would find this charming spot. In 1924, Winston Churchill purchased **Chartwell** as a family home and, with its magnificent views looking out over the Kentish Weald, it is easy to see why the great statesman said of Chartwell "I love the place - a day

away from Chartwell is a day wasted." From the 1920s until his death in the 1960s, Churchill lived here with his wife and the rooms have been left exactly as they were when the couple were alive: daily newspapers lie on the table, fresh flowers from the garden decorate the rooms and a box of his famous cigars lie ready. Meanwhile, the museum and exhibition rooms contain numerous mementoes from Churchill's extraordinary life and political career whilst the garden studio contains many of his paintings along with his easel and paintbox.

The gardens too have been well maintained, just as they were during his lifetime, and here visitors can see not only the golden rose walk that the couple's children planted on the occasion of Sir Winston and Lady Churchill's 50th wedding anniversary but also the brick wall that Churchill built with his own hands. The house is now in the ownership of the National Trust and it remains a wonderful, touching and lasting tribute to one of the country's most remarkable men.

WESTERHAM
10 miles NW of Tonbridge on the A25

A pleasant, small town close to the Surrey border, the building of the M25 close by has eased the town's traffic congestion and it is now a quieter and calmer place that is more in keeping with its former days as a coaching station. Along the town's main street and around the tiny green are a number of old buildings, including two venerable coaching inns, whilst, in the town centre, by the green, are two statues of British heroes who had connections with Westerham.

Chartwell

Squerryes Court

The first dates from 1969 and it is a tribute to Sir Winston Churchill, who made his home close by at Chartwell, and the other statue is that of General James Wolfe, who defeated the French at Quebec in 1759. Wolfe was born in Westerham and his childhood home, renamed **Quebec House**, can be found to the east of the town centre. Dating from the 17th century, this gabled red brick building, is now in the hands of the National Trust and here can be found portraits, prints and other memorabilia relating to the family, the general and his famous victory over the French.

Close by lies another historic house, **Squerryes Court** that too has connections with General Wolfe. Dating from 1681, this manor house was the home of the Warde family who were friends of Wolfe. Today, the house is home to an important collection of 18th century English and 17th century Dutch paintings as well as some splendid furniture, porcelain and tapestries. The grounds, including the formal gardens that are being restored in the 18th century style, are also well worth visiting (see panel below).

SQUERRYES COURT

Westerham, Kent TN16 1SJ
Tel: 01959 562345/563118 Fax: 01959 565949

There has been a house on the site that is now occupied by **Squerryes Court** since 1216 and, in 1658, when the diarist John Evelyn visited the medieval mansion he wrote the following description: "A pretty, finely wooded, well watered seate, the stables good, the house old but convenient." However, this building was not to last much longer as, in 1681, the then owner, Sir Nicholas Crisp, pulled it down and built in its place the glorious red brick house seen today. Bought by the Warde family in 1731, it remains in their hands today and Squerryes Court is perhaps best known for the important collection of 18th century English and 17th century Dutch paintings housed here - many of which were commissioned by the family. Meanwhile, there are also sumptuously decorated rooms that are home some splendid furniture, porcelain and tapestries. Of interest to military historians in Squerryes Court's connections with General Wolfe. The families were friends and it was whilst here that, at the age of 14 James Wolfe received his first commission in 1741 and one of the rooms has been set aside to display mementoes relating to the General. Outside lie the superb gardens that, following the Great Storm of 1987, have been restored to their original formal state using a garden plan of 1719 as a guide. Beyond lie the less formal landscaped grounds and parkland that was laid out in the mid 18th century.

2 North Kent Coast

From Margate, on the northeastern most tip of Kent, to Rochester, on the River Medway, the north Kent coast possesses a history that is inextricably linked with the sea. The whole area was invaded, over 2,000 years ago, by the Romans and, ever since, the land, villages and towns have played host to visitors from far afield and overseas. Many of the place names, such as Rochester and Whitstable, are derived from Saxon origins and, along with a Norman heritage, this area of coastline is, perhaps, one of the most interesting and historic in the whole of England.

The cathedral at Rochester was built, on a Saxon site, by William the Conqueror's architect, Bishop Gundulph, and it was also he who designed the massive fortress of Rochester Castle. Whilst this ancient city, with numerous connections with Charles Dickens, is one of the best known places along the Medway, it is Chatham that really captures the imagination. Henry VIII, looking to increase his sea power, established a dockyard at this originally Saxon settlement and, unknowingly, this was the beginning of the Royal Navy that was to be instrumental in the building and maintenance of the British Empire. The Naval Dockyards at Chatham, where Nelson's ship *HMS Victory* was built, along with the Napoleonic fortress, Fort Amherst, are two of the best monuments to the great seafaring traditions of the whole country. Meanwhile, in conjunction with the naval loyalties of Chatham, Gillingham is the home of the Royal Engineers and their museum highlights the valuable work that the Corps has done over the centuries in many areas, including civil engineering and surveying.

Further east lie the seaside towns and resorts of Whitstable, Herne Bay and Margate. Certainly the most popular is Margate, the natural destination for many people of southeast London looking for a day beside the sea. Whilst offering all the delights of the seaside, such as amusements, a fun fair, candyfloss and fish and chips, Margate is older than it seems and, with seaside fun in mind, it is not surprising that the bathing machine was invented in the town. Meanwhile, Whitstable, which remains famous for its oysters, presents a calmer and

Kingsgate Castle, nr Margate

less brash appearance to those looking for a seaside break. With a history that goes back to Roman times, this fishing village, that became the haunt of smugglers, has managed to retain an individuality that was to inspire writers such as Somerset Maugham and Charles Dickens.

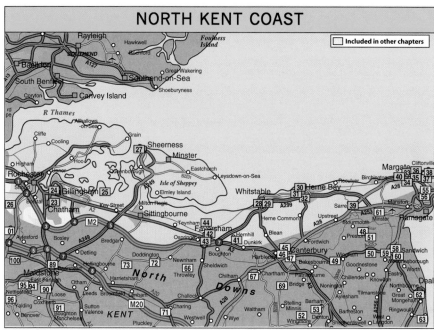

© MAPS IN MINUTES ™ (2000)

PLACES TO STAY, EAT, DRINK AND SHOP

ROCHESTER

First impressions of this riverside city are misleading as the pedestranised main shopping area and steady flow of traffic hide a history that goes back over 2,000 years. Rochester was first settled by the Romans, whose Watling Street crossed the River Medway at this point, and, to protect this strategic crossing point, they fortified their camp here and, in so doing, created a walled city of some 23 acres. Some five centuries later the Saxons arrived and it was at this time that the town acquired the name - Hrofesceaster - that, with some alteration over the years, became permanent. Still an important strategic town and port, it was at

River Medway

Rochester that King Alfred, determined to thwart Viking sea power, built a fleet of ships and thereby created the first English navy.

Following the Norman invasion in 1066, William the Conqueror, also aware of the importance of the town and its port, decreed that a castle be maintained here permanently and put his architect, Bishop Gundulph, to the task of designing a suitable fortification. Still dominating the city today, **Rochester Castle** is recognised to be one of the finest

surviving examples of Norman architecture in England. Over 100 feet tall and with walls that are around 12 feet thick, this massive construction comprised four floors from which there were many look out points. Despite the solidity of the fortress, it has had a very chequered history and, over the centuries, was subjected to three sieges. In particular, there is the siege that took place in 1215, when the rebellious barons were held here by King John for seven weeks. The barons withheld despite being bombarded by missiles thrown from huge siege engines and it was only when the props of a siege tunnel were burnt away and the tunnel collapsed that the barons surrendered. The collapsing of the tunnel also caused the massive tower above to collapse and this was later reconstructed, although in a round form rather than the original square shape, which now gives the castle its odd appearance. Rochester castle was again severely damaged during the Civil War and much of the building seen today is the result of restoration work undertaken in the 19th century.

As well as ordering the construction of the massive fortification, William the Conqueror also put his architect to the task of building **Rochester Cathedral** on the site of a Saxon church that was founded in AD 604. Today's building still contains the remains of the 12th century chapter house and priory, along with other Norman features, that, in particular, include the fine west doorway. Like the castle, the cathedral was badly damaged during the Civil War and restoration work was undertaken by the Victorians. The remains of former monastic buildings surround the cathedral and there are three ancient gates: Prior's Gate, Deanery Gate and Chertsey's Gate, that lead on to the High Street.

Found in the city's main street, not far from Rochester Bridge, is the **Guildhall Museum** that covers the history of this city from prehistoric times through to the mid 20th century. Along with the reconstruction of a room from the turn of the 19th century and other domestic items from the Victorian and Edwardian eras, the museum has many exhibits that relate to Rochester's maritime history. There are scale models of local sailing barges, a diorama of the Dutch raid of the Medway in 1667 and a reconstruction of one of the Medway prison hulks that were home to Napoleonic prisoners-of-war and other convicts.

Rochester Castle

Whilst the castle, cathedral and river certainly dominate Rochester, the city is perhaps most famous for its connections with the great Victorian novelist, Charles Dickens. The **Charles Dickens Centre**, housed in an Elizabethan building that Dickens knew well, brings to life the characters and places of his novels through the use of the latest technology. The grim reality of life in Victorian times is highlighted and world events of that age all go to help visitors put the stories of the novels in context. Meanwhile, outside in the garden is the fabricated chalet that Dickens had brought from Switzerland and placed in his own garden so that he could write in peace and quiet. Like many places in and around Rochester, this building in which the centre is housed featured in his novels: it

was Westgate House in *The Pickwick Papers* and The Nun's House in *The Mystery of Edwin Drood*, Dickens last and unfinished work.

There are many other buildings in the city with a Dickens' connection that are well worth seeking out. **The Royal Victoria and Bull Hotel**, that remains a hotel and restaurant today, featured as The Bull in *The Pickwick Papers* and again in *Great Expectations* as The Blue Boar. The addition of the 'Royal Victoria' to the hotel's name came in the 1830s following a visit here by the as yet uncrowned Queen Victoria, who was prevented from continuing to London by a violent storm in 1836. Much earlier, in 1573, Elizabeth I stayed in Rochester at the mansion house belonging to Richard Watts MP. Although now little remains of the building, Elizabeth was said to be so satisfied with the hospitality extended to her that the house became known as Satis House - a name that Dickens used, years later, in *Great Expectations*.

The busy port here and the routes to and from London that pass through Rochester have always ensured that the city has a steady stream of visitors and travellers passing through. And, after 11 years in exile, Charles II found himself staying overnight at Rochester whilst making his triumphal march from Dover to London in 1660. The mansion in which he found overnight hospitality was renamed Restoration House following the visit. On a less happy note, it was at Abdication House (now a bank on the High Street) that James II, fleeing from William of Orange in 1689, spent his last night in England.

AROUND ROCHESTER

UPNOR
2 miles NE of Rochester off the A228

With a river frontage along the Medway and a backdrop of wooded hills, Upnor became something of a resort for the people of the Medway towns. However, whilst this is indeed an ideal place to spend some leisure time, the village has not always been so peaceful. In the 16th century, Elizabeth I ordered the construction of several fortifications along the Medway estuary to protect her dockyard at Chatham from invasion and, in 1559, **Upnor Castle** was constructed. Fronted by a water bastion jutting out into the River Medway, this castle saw action in 1667 when the Dutch sailed up the river with the intention of destroying the English naval fleet. The gun batteries at Upnor were the primary defence against this attack but they proved to be ineffective as the Dutch captured, and made off with, the British flag ship the *Royal Charles*.

After this failure, the castle became a magazine and, at one time, more

gunpowder was stored here than at the Tower of London. One of the guns that failed to stop the Dutch has been salvaged from the river and now stands guard outside the entrance to the fort and visitors here can tour the gatehouse and main body of the castle.

Just up the river lies the **Royal Engineers' Upnor Base** where the testing and development of numerous devices and pieces of equipment relating to sea warfare took place.

COOLING
4½ miles N of Rochester off the A228

This isolated village lies on the Hoo peninsula that is characterised by its bleak marshland which lies between the Medway and the Thames. In 1381, John de Cobham of Cooling applied to Richard II to be granted the right to fortify his manor house as, at that time, the sea came right up to his house and he feared a seaborne attack. His fear was very much justified as, a couple of years earlier, the French had sailed up the river and set alight several villages in the area and the king was happy to allow the construction to go ahead. The result of de Cobham's work, which became known as **Cooling Castle**, can still be seen clearly from the road (although it is not open to the public) but the sea has receded over the years and no longer laps the castle's massive outer walls. In the 15th century, Cooling Castle became the home of Sir John Oldcastle, Lord of Cooling, who was executed in 1417 for the part he played in a plot against Henry V. Shakespeare is said to have modelled his character, Falstaff, on Sir John.

Close by the substantial castle remains stands **St James' Church** where, in the graveyard, there can be seen the 13 lozenge-shaped stones that mark the graves of various Comport children who all died of malaria in the 18th century. Not one of the children lived to be older than 17 months and these were, supposedly, the graves of Pip's brothers in Dickens' novel *Great Expectations*.

ALLHALLOWS
8 miles NE of Rochester off the A228

This remote village, that takes its name from its small 11th century church of All Saints, overlooks the River Thames estuary and, beyond, the busy Essex resort of Southend. Nearby, is an **Iron Beacon** that was erected in Elizabethan times and it is one of many such beacons that were set up along the coast to warn of imminent invasion. In the 1930s there were plans to develop the land to the north of the village, along the coast, as a holiday area and, although the resort never quite came to fruition, the Art Deco style railway station still remains and has been put to other uses.

GRAIN
10 miles NE of Rochester off the A228

This easternmost tip of the Hoo Peninsula is known as the **Isle of Grain** and from here there are sweeping views out across the Thames estuary but many are put off by the sight (and sometimes the smell) of the oil refineries and the power station that lie close by. It was from here that, along with many others, Sir Winston Churchill learned to fly from Grain's airfield.

CHATHAM
1 mile E of Rochester on the A2

Although there has been a settlement here since Saxon times, it was not until Henry VIII established a dockyard here that Chatham grew from being a sleepy, riverside backwater into the busy town of today. The dockyard flourished and it was expanded by Elizabeth I during the time

of the Armada. Sir Francis Drake, who took part in the defeat of the Spanish fleet in 1588, moved here with his family at the age of six and, whilst his father was chaplain to the fleet based here, the young Francis learned his sailing skills on the reaches around Chatham and Gillingham. Of the many famous ships that were built at the naval dockyard, perhaps the most famous is Nelson's *HMS Victory* which was launched in 1765.

The naval connection lay behind the steady growth of the town and its present commercial centre originally saw to the needs of navy personnel. Among these was John Dickens, who was employed by the Navy Pay Office and his son, Charles, spent some of his boyhood years at Chatham. The family moved to **2 Ordnance Terrace** (now number 11) when Charles was five and it was his father who was to provide the inspiration for the character Mr Micawber in *David Copperfield*.

Clocktower, Chatham Docks

Covered Building Slip, 1838

Just to the north of the town centre and found on the banks of the River Medway is the **World Naval Base**, Chatham's historic dockyard that was founded by Henry VIII and that was to become the premier shipbuilding yard for the Royal Navy. With over 400 years of history, there is plenty to see and do here and visitors can not only marvel at the scale of the 20th century submarine and battleship dry docked here but also the architecture - it is the most complete Georgian dockyard in the world (see panel below).

The Chatham dockyards were an obvious target for Hitler's bombers during World War II and, at **Fort Amherst Heritage Park and Caverns**, that lie close by, the secret underground telephone exchange, that co-ordinated the air raid warnings, can be seen. The country's premier Napoleonic fortress, Fort Amherst

WORLD NAVAL BASE

The Historic Dockyard, Chatham, Kent ME4 4TZ
Tel: 01634 823800 Fax: 01634 823801
e-mail: info@worldnavalbase.org.uk
website: www.worldnavalbase.org.uk

On the banks of the River Medway, lies the **World Naval Base** - Chatham's historic dockyard - that saw the foundation of the Royal Navy under Henry VIII and, down the centuries, it was the naval power generated here that helped build the British Empire. The Naval Base covers some 400 years of history and visitors touring the site will see the most complete Georgian dockyard in the world along with displays and exhibits that explain the part the dockyard has played in the country's and the world's history. Samuel Pepys, the famous diarist, first made reference to the dockyard in his diaries in 1661 and he was here to witness the audacious Dutch raid six years later when de Ruyter managed to capture the English flag ship, Royal Charles.

Whilst the dockyard exhibitions certainly dwell on past glories, there is plenty more to see here, including the modern spy submarine Ocelot, HMS Cavalier that saw active service during World War II and HMS Gannet the last surviving sloop of the Victorian navy. In a building that is a quarter of a mile long rope can be seen being made in the traditional way whilst the 175 year history of the lifeboats is told at the National Collection of the RNLI. The newly opened Museum of the Dockyard brings together the 400 year history of the World Naval Base and, with so much to see, the steam railway with its audio tour is an excellent way to begin a tour of this impressive site.

was built in 1756 to defend the naval dockyard from attack by land and it continued to serve this purpose up until the end of World War II. Today, the fort offers visitors an insight into the daily lives of the soldiers that were stationed here, and their families, through a series of displays and through re-enactments in period costumes. The fort's most outstanding feature, and most interesting, is undoubtedly the underground maze of tunnels and caverns that were used as storage, magazines, barracks and guardrooms and the guided tour around the underground workings highlights the skills of the military engineers.

Meanwhile, the extensive outer fortification, that covers seven acres and includes battlements and earthworks, has been turned into a country park style area where visitors can enjoy a picnic or walk the various nature trails. Again, like the dockyard, Fort Amherst has been used as a location by both film and television companies and it was here that Robert de Niro shot the prison cell scenes for *The Mission*, Val Kilmer worked on the remake of the 1960s series *The Saint* and the BBC filmed *The Phoenix and the Carpet*.

Found in a former church, opposite the fort, is the **Medway Heritage Centre** where every aspect of this working river is explored, including the lives of the men and women who worked on the banks and sailed on the water. Back in the main

part of the town can be found the **Almshouses** that were built by one of the two charities that were established by the Elizabethan seafarer, Admiral Sir John Hawkins. As well as helping to defeat the Spanish Armada along with Sir Francis Drake, Hawkins was also an inventor and philanthropist and it was he who introduced 'copper bottoms' to help prevent the deterioration of ship's hulls below the waterline. These almshouse at Chatham were originally designed as a hospital for retired seamen and their widows.

GILLINGHAM
2 miles E of Rochester on the A2

Although there is evidence of both prehistoric and Roman occupation of this area, a village did not really become established here until the 11th century. The oldest part of this, the largest of the Medway towns, is **The Green** and here can be found the Norman parish church of St Mary that dates from the early 12th century. However, it was the establishment of the dockyard at neighbouring Chatham in the 16th century that saw Gillingham begin to expand as it became a centre for servicing the naval dockyard and depot. As with many towns along the Medway, Gillingham has many links with the sea and it was the story of the Gillingham sailor, Will Adams, that inspired the novel

THE ROYAL ENGINEERS MUSEUM

Prince Arthur Road, Gillingham, Kent ME4 4UG
Tel: 01634 406397

The Royal Engineers Museum is like no other military museum and it reflects the diverse range of skills that the Corps has brought to bear both in peace time and war. The creators of the Ordnance Survey, the designers of the Royal Albert Hall and the founders of the Royal Flying Corps in 1912, the Royal Engineers continue the dangerous work of bomb disposal and throughout the world they build roads and bridges, lay water pipes and assisted in natural disasters. The new courtyard display illustrates the wide variety of activities the Corps has undertaken since the 1940s whilst, inside, there is a dignified medal gallery, a reconstruction of a World War I trench and numerous artefacts from around the world that have been acquired by members of the Corps.

Shogun by James Clavell. In 1600, Adams sailed to Japan and there he befriended Ieyasu, the Shogun, learnt Japanese and was honoured as a Samurai warrior. Found beside the A2 is the **Will Adams Monument**, a fitting tribute to the man who went on to become the Shogun's teacher and adviser.

Whilst all things maritime have certainly influenced Gillingham greatly over the centuries, the town is also the home of one of the most fascinating military attractions - **The Royal Engineers Museum**. (see panel opposite). Both the nearby dockyards and Fort Amherst, at Chatham, were built by the Royal Engineers and this superb museum tells of the diverse work of the Corps in both wartime and peacetime. Here visitors can see the original battlefield map prepared by the Corps and used by the Duke of Wellington to defeat Napoleon at the Battle of Waterloo in 1815. It was a Royal Engineer, Lieutenant John Chard VC, who played a key role in the defence of Rorkes Drift when the mission, with just 130 men, was attacked by thousands of Zulu warriors. More recently, the World War I General, Lord Kitchener, of the famous recruitment poster campaign, was also a Royal Engineer.

MILTON REGIS
10 miles SE of Rochester off the A2

Once a royal borough, Milton Regis has been all but incorporated into the outskirts of Sittingbourne. However, in the still well defined village centre can be found the **Court Hall Museum** housed, as its name might suggest, in a 15th century timbered building that was originally Milton Regis's courthouse, school and town gaol. The museum has displays, photographs and documents that relate to the village and surrounding area.

THE BARN YARD

Gore Farm, Oak Lane, Upchurch,
Sittingbourne, Kent ME9 7BE
Tel: 01634 235059/388856
website: www.the-barnyard.co.uk

Found just outside Upchurch, **The Barn Yard** is a place with a difference that has something for everyone. Owned and personally run by Mike and Susan Blee, with the help of their son Jamie, in 1988 the family rescued a series of derelict farm buildings from Herefordshire. After carefully dismantling the buildings, including a magnificent 17th century barn, they were moved to this site and re-erected.

Today the beautifully restored buildings house a range of farm shops lying in the heart of some of Kent's most glorious countryside. The Farm Shop offers a large selection of fruit and vegetables, including those grown on Gore Farm; there is a Pantry with it wide selection of tempting goods such as preserves, mustards and biscuits; a cheese shop and a gift shop that stocks all manner of unusual gifts that generally have a countryside theme.

The Gore Farm trails around this modern fruit farm also take in the traditional wild flower meadow, visitors can also take advantage of the farm's pick your own fruit throughout the spring and summer and, finally, there is a popular coffee shop here that specialises in home-made soups, cream teas and home-baked cakes.

Meanwhile, at **Milton Creek**, lies **Dolphin Yard Sailing Barge Museum** that lies in a traditional sailing barge yard where commercial work is still undertaken. Along with aiming to preserve the barges and other craft that have been used on the local estuaries for hundreds of years, the museum is also dedicated, in particular, to the sailing barge. While the creek provided a means of transport its waters were also used to power paper mills and paper manufacturing remains in evidence in this area today.

SITTINGBOURNE
10½ miles SE of Rochester on the A2

Lying close to the Roman road, Watling Street, Sittingbourne was, during the Middle Ages, a stopping place for pilgrims on their way to Canterbury. As a result of this the town developed a thriving market that has not been lost to this day and, along with the town's links with sailing barges, it is also a centre for paper manufacturing.

Another form of transport that was, at one time, much more common, is the steam train and from here the **Sittingbourne and Kemsley Light Railway** runs steam hauled passenger trains along two miles of preserved track. The railway was originally designed to transport paper and other bulk materials but now the journey is taken for pleasure by those fascinated by steam trains and those wishing to view this area of the Kentish countryside at close quarters.

BORSTAL
1½ miles S of Rochester off the B2097

Found on the eastern side of the elegant **Medway Bridge**, that carries the M2 over the River Medway, this is the village that

THE NEW BELL INN

126 High Street, Halling,
near Rochester,
Kent ME2 1BZ
Tel: 01634 240523
Fax: 01634 240523
e-mail: ronmoc@hotmail.com

Found close to the ancient village church, **The New Bell Inn** takes its name from the church bells and at one time it was called the Five Bells.

Very much a village pub, The New Bell has plenty of space within its two bars for locals to catch up on the latest news whilst, to the rear, there is a patio area and terraced garden that is much used in the summer. As well as keeping a good stock of real ales, beers, lagers and all the usual drinks for customers to quench their thirst, landlords, Ron and Christine, also offer an extensive menu of bar snacks and meals that range of cheese on toast and sandwiches to steaks and chicken fajita.

Throughout the year there are special themed evenings that prove very popular and, again looking to extend their hospitality, Ron and Christine organise a range of events such as quiz nights and golf and football teams. A friendly and down to earth local where those passing through the area, or walking the Pilgrims Way, can be sure of a warm welcome.

gave its name to young offenders institutions when the first prison of this type was opened here in 1908. The original borstal buildings can still be seen.

STROOD
1 mile W of Rochester off the A228

Situated on the opposite bank of the River Medway from Rochester, it was here that, during the Roman invasion of Britain masterminded by Claudius from Richborough, the Roman legions were halted by a force of Britons led by Caratacus. After two days, the Romans won the battle but only after Claudius had ordered some of his men to swim the river whilst others crossed higher up and surprised the Britons from behind.

However, it is as the home of **Temple Manor** that Strood is better known. Built in the 13th century by the Knights Templar, this was originally a hostel where the knights could find shelter, food and fresh horses whilst going to and from the Crusades. A building of simple design, this is all that survives from an earlier complex that would also have contained stables, kitchens and barns. Later, it became a nunnery that was dissolved under Henry VIII and eventually a farmhouse before falling into disrepair. Sympathetically restored after World War II, the original 13th century hall, with its vaulted undercroft, and the 17th century brick extensions have all survived.

A local legend tells that, during the bitter feuding between Henry II and Archbishop Thomas à Becket, the men of Strood, who were loyal to the king, cut off the tail of Becket's horse whilst he was riding through the town. Becket suggested that the descendants of those involved in the incident would be born with tails and so, apparently, they were!

As with other Medway towns, Strood has its connections with the sea and,

moored at the Kingsnorth Industrial estate nearby, is **The Medway Queen**, an old ship that was one of the many thousands that took part in the evacuation of Dunkirk in 1941.

HIGHAM
3 miles NW of Rochester off the A226

This scattered village, with its ancient and charming marshland church, is famous for being the home of Charles Dickens - the great novelist lived with his family at **Gad's Hill Place** from 1857 until his death in 1870. Originally dating from 1780, Dickens made various alterations to the house to accommodate his family and, in particular, he added a conservatory that, in 1995, was restored to its former glory. Whilst living at Gad's Hill, Dickens wrote several of his novels and he died before he could complete *The Mystery of Edwin Drood*. Although the house is now a school, some of the rooms and the grounds that Dickens so loved are open to the public at various times throughout the year. Visitors can see the study where he worked on his novels, the restored conservatory and stroll around the grounds.

MINSTER

This unprepossessing seaside town, situated on the northern coast of the Isle of Sheppey, is an unlikely place to find one of the oldest sites of Christianity in England. However, it was here, on the highest point of the island, that Sexburga, the widow of a Saxon king of Kent, founded a nunnery in the late 7th century. Sacked by the Danes in 855, **Minster Abbey** was rebuilt in around 1130 when it was also re-established as a priory for Benedictine nuns. Sometime later, in the 13th century, the parish church of Minster was built, adjoining the monastic church, and so, from the Middle Ages until the Dissolution of the Monasteries, the building served as a 'double church' with the nun's worshipping in the northern half of the building and the parishioners in the other. To the west of this unusual church lies the 15th century abbey gatehouse that, today, is home to the **Minster Abbey Gatehouse Museum**. Here, there are displays on the history of Sheppey which is told through exhibits of fossils, tools and photographs.

In his *Ingoldsby Legends*, RH Barham retells the story of the fiery Sir Roger de Shurland, Lord of Sheppey who, in 1300, killed a monk who had disobeyed him.

Minster Abbey Gatehouse

Dodging the county sheriff, Sir Roger swam out on horseback to Edward I's passing ship and received the king's pardon for his wicked act. On returning to shore, Sir Roger met a mysterious old hag who foretold that, having saved his life, Sir Roger's horse would also cause his death. On hearing this, the tempestuous knight drew his sword and beheaded his horse. Some time later, whilst walking on the beach, Sir Roger came across the head of his horse that had been washed ashore. In an angry rage, he kicked the head but

one of the horse's teeth penetrated his boot and Sir Roger died later from the infection that developed in the wound. Sir Roger's tomb lies in the abbey church and close to the right foot of his stone effigy can be seen the head of a horse.

AROUND THE ISLE OF SHEPPEY

EASTCHURCH
2½ miles SE of Minster off the B2231

This village was once the home of the early pioneers of aviation and, not only did a young Sir Winston Churchill fly from the old Eastchurch aerodrome, but another early pilot, Lord Brabazon of Tara, was the holder of Pilot's Licence No 1. Close to the church is a stone memorial to the early pilots whilst, nearby, are the ruins of 16th century Shurland Hall, where Henry VIII and Anne Boleyn stayed on their honeymoon.

A little outside the village lies **Norwood Manor** a charming old house that dates from the 17th century although the 'Northwoode' family have lived on this site since Norman times. On display in the house are numerous artefacts that relate to this long established Kentish family.

LEYSDOWN
5 miles SE of Minster on the B2231

A popular seaside place with visitors for many years - Henry VIII loved the Isle of Sheppey so much that he spent one of his honeymoons here - Leysdown is renowned for its sandy beaches while there are picnic areas and nature trails close by.

A little to the south, and found on the southeastern tip of the Isle of Sheppey, **The Swale National Nature Reserve** is home to numerous wildfowl and visitors here can combine watching the birds with coastal walking.

ELMLEY ISLAND
3 miles S of Minster off the A249

Situated on southern coastline of the Isle of Sheppey and overlooking The Swale and the north Kent coast, **Elmley Marshes Nature Reserve** is an area of salt marsh that is home to wetland birds, marsh frogs, numerous insects and many species of aquatic plants.

QUEENBOROUGH
3 miles W of Minster off the A249

An historic town that began as a Saxon settlement, Queenborough became an important wool port and a wealthy borough that was graced by a royal **Castle** built here by Edward III. The town's reliance on the sea for its prosperity also saw its courthouse captured by the Dutch during their invasion of the Medway in 1667 and, later, during World War II, Queenborough saw another invasion, this time when it became the home of

hundreds of mine-sweeping vessels. **The Guildhall Museum**, that is housed in the building that replaced the earlier courthouse, tells the fascinating story of this town, from Saxon times, through its rise at the hands on Victorian industrialists, to the important role Queenborough played during World War II.

SHEERNESS
2½ miles NW of Minster on the A249

Overlooking the point where the River Medway meets the River Thames, Sheerness was once the site of a naval dockyard and it was the first to be surveyed, in the 17th century, by Samuel Pepys, the famous diarist, who held the position of Secretary of the Admiralty during the reign of Charles II. It was at Sheerness that, in 1805, *HMS Victory* docked when it brought Nelson's body back to England after the Battle of Trafalgar. In more recent times, Sheerness has developed into a busy container and car ferry port and most of the Isle of Sheppey's wealth is centred on the town.

The **Sheerness Heritage Centre** is housed in a 19th century dockyard worker's cottage that has been decorated and furnished in genuine 19th century style. There is also an exhibition here on the history of the dockyard and its influence in the development of the town (see panel below).

SHEERNESS HERITAGE CENTRE

10 Rose Street, Sheerness, Kent
Tel: 01795 663317

The Sheerness Heritage Centre is housed in a weatherboarded cottage that was built in the early 19th century as a dwelling for a dockyard worker. Despite being constructed of seemingly temporary building materials the house, as with its two neighbours, has lasted well and, over the years, it has also been a baker's shop and a fish and chip shop. Now cared for, the rooms here have been restored and they now reflect authentic 19th century rooms and are furnished with genuine pieces from that period. The Royal Dockyard here closed in the 1960s - it has now become a flourishing port - and, in the heritage centre, there is also an exhibition describing the development of the dockyard along with a display of tools used by its workers.

WHITSTABLE

Anyone wandering around Whitstable will soon realise that this is no seaside resort but very much a working town that is centred around the busy commercial harbour that was originally the port for Canterbury. The old fashioned streets of the town are lined with fisherman's cottages and the winding lanes are linked by narrow alleyways with eccentric names - such as **Squeeze Gut Alley** - that recall the town's rich maritime past. Sometimes referred to as the "Pearl of Kent", Whitstable is as famous today for its oysters as it was in Roman times and it is probable that Caesar himself enjoyed Whitstable oysters. Eaten in the best restaurants in London and further a field, Wheelers Oyster bar in the town is one survivor of the numerous bars that were once here where the oysters can be enjoyed, along with other fish, fresh from the sea.

After the Roman occupation left Britain, the Saxons came to the area and it is they who gave the town its name; then Witanstaple, meaning 'an assembly of wise men in the market', which later became Whitstable. Later, the Normans built the parish church of All Saints, which provided medieval sailors with a key navigation aid, although the ownership of the manor of Whitstable in the Middle Ages proved to be something of a poisoned chalice: John de Stragboli was executed for murder; Bartholomew de Badlesmere was hanged for his part in the rebellion against Edward II and Robert de Vere was convicted for treason. Even during reign of Henry VIII in the 16th century, the owner of the manor faired no better and Sir John Gates was executed for his support of Lady Jane Grey over the Catholic Mary Tudor.

THE HARBOUR ST CAFÉ

48 Harbour Street, Whitstable, Kent CT5 1AQ
Tel: 01227 772575
website: www.harbourstreetcafe@fsnet.com

Found on Whitstable's main street, **The Harbour St Café** occupies a corner site that ensures that the interior of this interesting restaurant is light and airy.

Owned and personally run by Gillian Reckitt and her daughter Josephine, since late 1999, The Harbour St Café specialises in vegetarian and organic foods. Open all day, every day, the all day light menu includes several breakfast options as well as a list of sandwiches served with a choice of breads and home-made cakes. Meanwhile, there is another, more substantial menu served here that, thanks to Josephine's training as a chef, reflects tastes and styles from around the world.

On both Friday and Saturday evenings, The Harbour St Café also opens its doors when not only is the main menu available but, each month, there is also a special menu featuring dishes from a particular country or region around the globe. With a fine wine list - that too includes organic wines - and live music once a month, The Harbour St Café is not only interesting and imaginative but also an enjoyable place to eat.

Shell Fishing, Whitstable

Along with oysters and a fishing industry that has lasted over 700 years, the discovery of iron pyrites deposits around Whitstable led to the development of the manufacture of copperas that was used for dyeing, making ink and some early medicines. However, it was the sea and the associated boat building and repair yards that were to continue to support many of those living in the town. Now many of the yards have gone but, as recently as World War II,

ships' lifeboats and other small craft were being built and launched at Whitstable. Going hand in hand with the town's maritime connections was the unofficial trade of smuggling and, during the 18th century, there were numerous battles between the gangs and the revenue men in and around the town. Whilst the authorities clamped down hard on this illegal trading, there was one positive spin-off as the smugglers had such an intimate knowledge of the French coastline that Nelson consulted them whilst planning his naval campaigns.

Found on the harbour's East Quay is the **Oyster and Fishery Exhibition** that not only tells the story of Whitstable's connections with seafood and fish but it is here that visitors are able to see the first commercial oyster hatchery in the world. Naturally, there are fresh Whitstable

BEAU RIVAGE

101 Tankerton Road, Whitstable, Kent CT5 2AJ
Tel: 01227 272056 website: www.worldworx.net/beaurivage.htm

At a first glance **Beau Rivage**, on the outskirts of Whitstable, looks like most other neat, tidy and average small town restaurants but it would be a great mistake not to explore further. Owned and personally run by Gina and Neil Evans since the late 1980s, Beau Rivage is superb restaurant that treats its customers to an exceptional dining experience. Chef Neil has previously worked at both the Ritz Hotel and the Sheraton Park Tower in London and both the skills he has learnt and his own ability and dedication have gained both him and the restaurant a magnificent reputation and loyal following. In the restaurant's pleasant surroundings customers are treated to a menu that is based on classic French cuisine with modern overtones that also embraces the style of the Mediterranean and the Far East. The menu changes daily, depending on market availability and as well as the very reasonable set lunchtime menu there is always a fully evening à la carte. Booking is essential at the weekends and Beau Rivage is open Tuesday to Saturday throughout the year.

THE VICTORIA HOTEL

85 Central Parade, Herne Bay, Kent CT6 5JQ
Tel: 01227 369660 Fax: 01227 365425
e-mail: alan@victoria3460.freeserve.co.uk
website: www.victoriahotel.uk.com

Found close to Herne Bay's harbour and the
bandstand, **The Victoria Hotel** is a charming family
run hotel that caters for both holidaymakers and
business people alike. Over 100 years old, the hotel
has a small frontage on to Central Parade but this is
misleading as, inside, the building is surprisingly
spacious .

Owners Alan Watson and his daughter Clare
Sidders offer all their guests a warm and friendly
welcome and there is a choice of seven guest rooms -
ranging from a honeymoon suite to twin rooms - that
are all comfortable and, although not all have en suite
facilities, they do have plenty to make guests feel at
home. A full English breakfast is served in the dining
room and, as the centre of the town is within five
minutes walk, there is lots of choice of restaurant for
an evening meal.

However, The Victoria Hotel does have another
surprise for guests as there is a heated indoor
swimming pool here as well as a sauna and sunbed. So whatever the English weather, Alan and Clare
can provide all that is needed for a good seaside holiday.

SHELLEY'S CAFÉ

116 High Street, Herne Bay, Kent CT10 5JY
Tel: 01227 740392

Found within Herne Bay's shopping centre, **Shelley's Café** is a light, bright and cheerful daytime café
that proves to be very popular with those shopping here. Completely refurbished in November 2000,
when Shelley Morgan bought the property, she, along with the help of her family, adopt a real hands
on approach to the café.

Open from 06.00 am until around 18.00 pm, Shelley's Café offers a full menu of tasty snacks and
light meals that begin with a choice of breakfast. To compliment this extensive menu there is a daily

specials board that is available
from 10.00 am onwards. Along
with favourites such as a mixed
grill, fish and chips and both hot
and cold sandwiches (that are
all prepared to order), Shelley's
has a list of traditional English
puddings that include a home-
made apple crumble.

Although this is the family's
first venture into the trade, the
stylish surroundings, good food
and the attention paid to
customer care ensures that the
café will continue to be as
popular as it has now become.

oysters and clams on the menu at the exhibition's café. Meanwhile, for a broader picture of the town, past and present, **Whitstable Museum and Gallery** explores the traditions and life of this ancient seafaring community. There are also references and information on the many 'firsts' to which the town lays claim: the first scheduled passenger train ran between Whitstable and Canterbury; the first steamship to sail to Australia from Britain left here in 1837; the diving helmet was invented in the town; and the country's first council houses were built at Whitstable.

However, not everyone is an inventor and visionary and, more recently, Whitstable has become fashionable with writers and those associated with the media industry. After his parents died, Somerset Maugham came to live with his uncle at Whitstable and the town features strongly in two of his novels, *Of Human*

Bondage and *Cakes and Ale*. Charles Dickens visited here and wrote about the town whilst Robert Hitchens, the novelist and journalist, lived nearby at Tankerton. One of the town's less celebrated residents was William Joyce who, before travelling to Germany to broadcast Nazi propaganda back to England as Lord Haw Haw, worked in one of the town's radio shops.

AROUND WHITSTABLE

HERNE BAY
4½ miles NE of Whitstable on the B2205

Now one of the main resorts on the north Kent coast, Herne Bay was, originally, a fishing village that became notorious as a haunt for smugglers. Much of the town seen today was laid out in the mid 19th century as it was developed as a resort to attract Victorian middle classes looking

HARBOUR BAR CAFÉ AND CONNAUGHT SOCIAL CLUB

98 Central Parade, Herne Bay, Kent CT6 5JJ
Tel: 01227 372128

Overlooking the seafront the **Harbour Bar Café** is an excellent place to stop and enjoy some delicious refreshments. Managed since 1998 by Arlene Fulcher, the café bar, which is open from 11.30 until late evening, has a stylish interior that helps to create the sophisticated atmosphere that characterises the establishment. Along with a full range of drinks served from the bar, the Harbour Bar Café serves an interesting menu of home-cooked dishes that vary in taste - from standard English favourites to

exotic dishes from around the world. Children too are welcome here.

Meanwhile, above the café bar is the Connaught Bingo and Social Club that is also ably managed by Arlene. Open to those who have been a member for over 24 hours, this fully licensed club provides plenty of seating in a light and airy room. Obviously a place for keen bingo players, those not so interested in the game will find that they can enjoy a drink and some food whilst watching the games.

for clean air and safe beaches. It still retains a quiet gentility that is reminiscent of that lost era and, at the **Herne Bay Museum Centre**, visitors can, through entertaining displays, discover the history of the town and the story of its famous pier. Meanwhile, the museum also contains relics from prehistoric times such as fossils and stone tools. Also in the town is a superb landmark, the **Clock Tower**, that stands on the promenade and was given to Herne Bay by a wealthy London lady to commemorate Queen Victoria's coronation in 1836.

Just inland, at the ancient Saxon village of **Herne**, stands **Herne Mill**, a Kentish smock mill that has recently undergone extensive repair work. Dating from 1789, this particularly mill is the latest in a long line that have occupied this site.

RECULVER
7½ miles NE of Whitstable off the A299

Reculver is the site of the Roman Regulbium, one of the forts built in the 3rd century to defend the shores of Kent from Saxon invasion. Sometime later the site was taken over as a place of Christian worship and this early fort provided the building materials for the 7th century Saxon church that was later extended by the Normans. It was also around this time that the Normans built the two huge towers, within the remains of the Roman fort, that provided mariners with a landmark to guide them into the Thames estuary. Today, **Reculver Towers and Roman Fort** that is under the management of English Heritage, has been preserved and, although there are only few remains of the fort, the towers still stand overlooking the rocky beach and can be seen from several miles along the coast. Meanwhile, **Reculver Country Park** offers visitors a lovely walk to these remains, church and towers and the park's

visitors centre has some fascinating information on the history and natural history of this stretch of coastline.

As a major historic site, Reculver has, of course, seen much archaeological activity over the years and, in the 1960s, an excavation unearthed several tiny skeletons that were buried not far from the towers. It is generally believed that these babies were buried alive as human sacrifices and, it is said, that on stormy nights the babies can be heard crying out.

BIRCHINGTON
12 miles E of Whitstable on the A28

This quiet resort, with cliffs and bays, still retains its individually despite the spread of the Margate conurbation from the east and it is a particular favourite for families with young children. At **All Saints' Church** there is a monument to one of the most famous British artists of the 19th century, Dante Gabriel Rossetti, the poet and artist who was instrumental in the formation of the Pre-Raphaelite Brotherhood. He lies buried in the doorway and a memorial stone, carved by his mentor, Ford Madox Brown, marks his grave.

About half a mile to the southeast of the village lies **Quex House**, a Regency gentleman's country house that was later expanded into the Victorian mansion seen today. It remains the home of the Powell-Cotton family and visitors looking around the rooms will find that the house still retains the atmosphere of a family home, complete with freshly cut flowers from the garden. A fine collection of period and oriental furniture, family portraits, porcelain and silver can also be seen by those wandering through the rooms. One particular member of the family, Major PHG Powell-Cotton, was a great explorer and whilst he was lured to exotic lands by big game, the Major was a

Westgate on Sea

tribal art, costumes and weapons to European and Chinese porcelains and local archaeological finds, there is a vast range of exhibits to be seen here from right around the world. As well as offering visitors a great deal to see inside the house, Quex is surrounded by a some superb **Gardens**, parkland and woodlands that provide the perfect backdrop to this fascinating house.

true Victorian who also took an interest in the customs and beliefs of the people and tribes that he met on his travels. As a result he put together a vast collection and the **Museum** here displays that collection in polished mahogany cases that also give the galleries an authentic quality. From dioramas of animals and

MARGATE
15 miles E of Whitstable on the A28

With its long stretch of golden sand, promenades, amusement arcades, candyfloss and fun fairs, Margate is very much everyone's idea of a boisterous English seaside resort. However, this is a reputation that has grown up for over 200

THE COTTAGE PUB AND STEAK HOUSE

19 High Street, Margate, Kent CT9 1DL
Tel: 01843 229119

Found on Margate's main street and close to the harbour, **The Cottage Pub and Steak House** is an interesting old building whose front façade dates from the mid 18th century although the back is older! The ground floor of

the building is the pub and here customers can choose from a good range of real

ales, many of which are locally brewed, as well as all the usual beers, lagers, ciders and spirits.

Owners, Tessa and John Tolley, have only been here since the autumn of 2000 and, in that short time, not only have they gained a reputation for the quality of the drinks served here but also for their cuisine. Beginning with breakfast, the menu here offers a wide range of dishes that include both traditional English favourites, curries and lighter snacks. However, John, an excellent cook, specialises in steaks and there is plenty of choice here.

Meanwhile, on the first floor is the restaurant that provides a more formal environment for dining and this is open for lunch from Friday to Sunday.

THE ROSE IN JUNE

49 Trinity Square, Margate, Kent CT9 1HT
Tel: 01843 280877

Found on Trinity Square, in a tucked away part of Margate, **The Rose in June** is a quaint old inn that has been offering hospitality to its customers for many years.

Stepping inside this attractive building is just like going back in time as the interior is very Victorian. Behind the solid wooden bar are a row of engraved mirrors that have, undoubtedly, been here for around 100 years and, along with the period light fittings and the rich decor, there is an authentic air of days gone by here.

However, whilst the quaint surroundings certainly hark back to yesteryear, the service here does not. Landlady, Rhona Barnett has over 60 years experience in the trade mainly at inns and pubs in the City of London and the West End so customer care comes as a second nature.

As well as ensuring that everyone, whether visitors or regulars, receive a warm and friendly welcome, Rhona has a well stocked bar that includes all the usual drinks along with a choice of Kent brewed real ales. A comfortable and popular inn there is live music here every Saturday evening.

DUG OUT RESTAURANT AND CAFÉ BAR

4 Fort Hill, Margate, Kent CT9 1HD
Tel: 01843 232117

Found in the old quarter of Margate and overlooking the harbour, the sunsets over which have been immortalised by the artist Turner, lies the **Dug Out Restaurant and Café Bar**. Very much a family run business, with Maria Ioannou at the helm, the family have been here since 1996 and, as well as completely refurbishing this interesting old building, they have certainly gained an enviable reputation for their high standard of service.

Housed within the vaults of an old brewery, the restaurant and café bar is open all day, every day, and among the many interesting dishes served here the Dug Out Restaurant specialises in steaks and

Mexican sizzling dishes. Children, too, are well catered for with their own menu that has a fixed price of just 99p. However, there is much more to this establishment as there is the Millennium Bar public house and a much used function room.

Meanwhile, those looking for somewhere to stay can also take advantage of the three family sized suites (each with their own bathroom) that are to be increased to nine by the end of 2001.

As well the reasonably priced accommodation Maria also arranges day trips from the here to France, again at very acceptable prices.

The Sands, Margate

again to wander the pleasant streets of the old town and take the bracing sea air. With this background as a seaside resort, it is not surprising to find that the bathing machine was invented here, in 1752, by a Quaker, glovermaker and a Margate resident called Benjamin Beale.

Whilst the town might seemingly be devoted to fun and the beach, there is more to Margate than candyfloss and fish and chips and, in King Street, can be found the **Tudor House** that years, not recently, and, before the railway brought holidaymakers in the droves from London from the 1840s onwards, those looking for a day by the sea came in sailing boats known as Margate hoys. Still often regarded as the first choice for a day out by those living in southeast London, many people return here time and time dates back to the early 16th century and the reign of Henry VIII. Meanwhile, just inland, lies the medieval **Salmestone Grange** that originally belonged to St Augustine's Abbey at Canterbury. Arguably, one of the best preserved examples of a monastic grange in England, the chapel, crypt and kitchen

THE DANE VALLEY

Dane Valley Road, Margate, Kent CT9 3RZ
Tel: 01843 223823

Situated on the outskirts of Margate, and with plenty of off road parking, **The Dane Valley** is a friendly inn that caters for regular customers as well as those passing through the area. Large, imposing and hard to miss, the interior of the inn has an altogether warmer and more personal feel whilst the open plan nature of the layout prevents the inn becoming over crowded even when it is busy. Landlords, Rosemary and Alan Goodship have plenty of experience in the licensing trade and, although they have only been here since spring 2000, they have certainly gained a following.

Along with the excellent range of drinks served at the bar, that includes a choice of real ales, a tasty menu of snacks, such as sandwiches and egg and chips, is served up until 18.00. A popular and friendly inn, there is always something happening here and, along with darts matches, there are regular discos where everyone is welcome.

During the summer customers spill out into the beer garden at the back of the inn and, by spring 2002, Rosemary and Alan also hope to be able to offer comfortable accommodation to families.

WALPOLE BAY HOTEL

Fifth Avenue, Cliftonville, Kent CT9 2JJ
Tel: 01843 221703 Fax: 01843 297399 website: www.walpolebayhotel.co.uk

Found along the sea front, in this resort that is well known for its bracing air and sunshine, lies the impressive **Walpole Bay Hotel**. The hotel dates from the Edwardian age and it was built at the time when Cliftonville was being developed into a fashionable resort that was particularly enjoyed by the wealthy from London and beyond. Today, the hotel continues to offer excellent hospitality to discerning guests and owners, Jane and Peter Bishop, ensure that the best traditions of a family run hotel are maintained. The Walpole Bay Hotel may

seem familiar to some guests as it has appeared in the BBC television programme *One Foot in the Past* on account of the many features that the building retains from the 1920s. In fact, it could be considered a living museum from that period and, throughout, there are reminders of those days. In particular, there is a delightful and fully functional, 1927 Otis trellis gated lift that still serves the hotel's five floors. The hotel's motto - "The elegance of a bygone era relived" - could not be nearer the truth.

The main reception rooms of the hotel are beautifully decorated and furnished to highlight the 1920s style of this elegant and charming hotel. There are numerous lounge

areas where guests can settle down with a good book or enjoy conversation whilst, before dinner, drinks can be taken in the bar. Dining at the hotel's Walpole Restaurant is also a treat not to be missed. Serving both lunches and dinners, and open to non residents, the dining room is yet another stylish and well appointed room that all adds to the hotel's atmosphere of gracious living. The menus here concentrate on British country cuisine with a modern day edge and each dish is prepared with flair and imagination. Throughout the year, the restaurant also hosts a number of gourmet evenings when the dishes follow the culinary traditions of one particular area or country from right around the world. Meanwhile, weather permitting, breakfast, light meals and the hotel's fabulous cream teas are served on the front sun terrace. A charming place to sit at any time of the day, the terrace, at the front of the hotel, has a wrought iron and glass canopy and plenty of comfortable wicker seating as well as fantastic panoramic views to offer guests. If the sea air becomes too bracing guests can retire to the spacious lounge where not only can they still

enjoy the hotel's wonderful hospitality but also sink into one of the many comfortable armchairs.

Each of the hotel's 42 en suite guest rooms - a combination of double, single and family suites - has a sea view with many also having balconies. Each has been individually decorated and furnished to bring out not only the room's original features that still remain, but also to provide each guest with a true feeling of personal service that is another key watchword here. Newly weds, or couples celebrating their anniversary, may

like to take advantage of one of the hotel's three beautiful bridal suites where pride of place is given to a grand four poster bed.

On all the floors of the hotel are exhibitions by local artists that include a picture gallery on the second floor, a display of photographs on the first floor and, on the ground floor, can be found Couture antiques. Meanwhile, other facilities found at the hotel include the ball room where tea dances, dinner dances and full range of evening events are held. This too is a popular local venue for annual dinners and functions as well as being used for wedding receptions - a hotel speciality. Those wishing to take the bracing north Kent coast air will find that, just outside the hotel, are the carefully attended lawns and formal gardens for which many English resorts are famous and the beach is only a short distance away. Golf is also a popular activity among many guests and the Walpole Bay Hotel organises special Golfing Breaks.

ST MALO HOTEL

Surrey Road, Cliftonville, Margate, Kent CT9 2LA
Tel: 01843 224931

Found in a quiet residential area between the beach and the town's main shopping area, the **St Malo Hotel** is ideally placed for those wishing to stay in this attractive part of Kent. Once a large Victorian house, the hotel is owned by Jill and Dave McMillan who, since they came here in late 2000, have put in a lot of work to put the place back on its feet. Newly decorated in a pleasing manner and comfortably furnished each of the guest rooms provides everything needed for a relaxing stay. Many of the guest rooms also have en suite bathrooms.

Whilst here, guests can make full use of the hotel's well established town garden and, in the evening, enjoy a drink and conversation in the bar. Accommodation here is on a bed and breakfast basis, with the additional option of dinner and the meals are served in the elegant dining room where there is also a choice of menu. A convenient and pleasant place to stay, out of season the St Malo Hotel offers a number of special break packages.

SARRE MILL

Canterbury Road, Sarre, near Birchington, Kent CT7 0JU
Tel: 01843 847573

Found on high ground just to the northeast of the village is one of the country's few remaining commercially working mills, **Sarre Mill**, a typical Kentish smock windmill. Built in 1820 by the Canterbury millwright John Holman, a steam engine was installed here in 1861 to add further power although it was not until the 1920s that the sails were taken down and the mill wheels were completely powered by the gas engine that was installed in 1907. Milling finally ceased at Sarre in the 1940s and, after being left derelict for decades, the building was purchased in 1985 by the Hobbs family and restoration work was begun.

Today, Sarre Mill is back to working order, producing high quality stoneground flour, and, as well as touring the five floors of the mill, there is plenty more for the whole family to see. There are small farmyard animals, including Victoria, a Tamworth pig, that are sure to delight children and a rare portable steam engine dating from the 1860s that was used to crush apples for cider making. Numerous other items of rural interest, such as old agricultural machinery, farming implements and domestic pieces, are on display here in the exhibition of bygones. A tea rooms provides visitors with the ideal opportunity to enjoy some home-made bread or cake, all made using Sarre Mill flour, whilst, at the mill shop, not only can the flour be purchased but also a wide range of other country goods.

Sunset, Margate

1930s, the mill was restored to working order in the 1970s.

SARRE
9 miles SE of Whitstable on the A28

This sunken village lies on the edge of marshland and it was, centuries ago, an important harbour and ferry when the Isle of Thanet was, indeed, an island. Today, it is home to one of the country's few remaining commercially working mills, **Sarre Mill**, a typical Kentish smock windmill that dates from 1820. The addition of first steam and then gas power ensured that Sarre Mill remained in use well into the 20th century but in the 1940s milling ceased here. Fortunately, in the 1980s, the windmill was restored and today not only does it continue to produce high quality stoneground flour but there is also a display here of rural artefacts, including a steam engine, that adds further interest to a visit to the windmill (see panel opposite).

HERNE COMMON
4 miles SE of Whitstable off the A291

Close to the village and found deep in a leafy forest is **Wildwood**, Kent's unique woodland discovery park that is also the

can all still be seen. Another building that has withstood the test of time is **Drapers Mill**, an old smock corn mill that was constructed in 1845 by John Holman. It continued to the powered by the wind until a gas engine was installed in 1916 and, after being made redundant in the

THE DOG AND DUCK HOTEL

44 Canterbury Road, Westbrook, Margate, Kent CT9 5BG
Tel: 01843 292358

Situated on the seafront and just a short walk from the centre of Margate, **The Dog and Duck Hotel** is an imposing red brick that is hard to miss. The original early Victorian building was demolished in the 1930s, when the road into Margate was widened and today's hotel, constructed at this time, still displays many features from that 'between the wars' era. A friendly and welcoming pub, hotel and restaurant, hosts Kate and Karl Limbert have certainly put their years of experience in the licensing trade to excellent use and customers here are sure to be treated to the very best hospitality. A full range of drinks is served at the bar where, too, a tempting range of bar snacks are also available throughout the day. The dining room, which overlooks the beer garden and then the beach, is a pleasant place to enjoy the extensive à la carte menu. Both children and dogs are welcome here and there is a selection of comfortable guest rooms, some of which overlook the beach.

THE RED LION

The Green, Hernhill, Faversham, Kent ME13 9JR
Tel: 01227 751207 Fax: 01227 752990
website: www.theredlionpub.co.uk

Standing opposite the village green is the impressive **Red Lion**, an old inn that was originally built as a Kentish hall house in 1364. A wonderfully attractive and atmospheric inn inside, there are stone floors, exposed brickwork and the timber beams, from which hang hop bines, that all add to the delights of this lovely inn.

Landlords, Stephen and Denise have been here since summer 1999 and they have certainly made their mark. As well as serving all manner of drinks from their well stocked bar, including several real ales, the couple have gained an excellent reputation for the high standard of cuisine on offer here.

The extensive menu, that contains a tempting selection of home-cooked dishes, is served both downstairs in the main area of the inn or upstairs in the splendid restaurant. Along with the wonderful food, the restaurant (for which booking is essential at the weekends) has a magnificent exposed beam ceiling that is well worth seeing.

There is a large rear beer garden that is much used in the summer and Stephen and Denise also offer accommodation in a two bedroom self-catering cottage that is as charming as the inn as well as having a full range of facilities.

THE HOLE IN THE WALL

75 Preston Street, Faversham, Kent ME13 8PA
Tel: 01795 591817

Found in the heart of Faversham, **The Hole in the Wall** is a quaint old inn that despite its small frontage has a surprisingly large and spacious interior. Full of olde worlde character and charm, with low timber beamed ceilings and exposed brickwork, this stylish inn is a popular place with both locals and visitors alike.

Landlord, Patrick O'Connell has plenty of experience in the trade, much of which he gained in London, and he and his staff certainly know how to look after their customers. Along with the choice of real ales and all the usual drinks served from the bar, including two draught ciders, The Hole in the Wall has an extensive lunchtime menu. A mouth-watering list of tasty favourites, the menu is supplemented by a daily specials board that ensures that everyone will be tempted by an interesting dish. Everything here is home-cooked and, by the end of 2001, an evening menu will also be available.

A charming place at anytime of the day, where children too are welcome, there is a disco here each Friday and Saturday evening.

home of the only breeding pack of endangered European wolves in Britain. Although wolves have not been living in the wild in this country for many years, tales of the savage packs that once roamed the countryside live on and, here, stories of the medieval hunters who killed them for bounty and of the fear of travellers alone on dark nights bring back those days. The Saxons called January 'Wulf monat' as this was when the hungry packs were at their most dangerous. However, Wildwood is not entirely devoted to wolves and here, in the forest, is a reconstruction of a Saxon village, Regia Anglorum, where living history is brought to life as village members, in authentic costume, go about their daily lives and practice the skills and crafts from centuries ago.

Other wildlife also abound at Wildwood and, along with the badger colony here there are rabbits, polecats, shrews and hedgehogs all living in underground burrows. Meanwhile, living in a near natural environment is the park's herd of deer. Whilst this is an interesting, enjoyable and educational place to visit for all the family, much of the work of the park goes on behind the scenes, in the area of conservation, and two species in particular, water voles and hazel dormice, are bred here for re-introduction into the wild.

HERNHILL
5 miles SW of Whitstable off the A299

A secluded and tranquil village that is surrounded by orchards, Hernhill is also home to **Mount Ephraim Gardens** that can be found on a family estate that also includes a house, woodland and fruit farm. There are magnificent views of both the Swale and Thames estuaries from the gardens which themselves offer a good balance between the formal and the

informal through such delights as herbaceous borders, topiary, rose terraces, a vineyard and orchard trails.

FAVERSHAM
6 miles SW of Whitstable on the A2

As with many places in this area of Kent, Faversham was first settled by the Romans, who gave the town its name (it comes from 'faber' meaning blacksmith), and it was later inhabited by both the Jutes and the Saxons. Despite this period of turmoil, the town continued to grow, so much so in fact that, in 811, King Kenulf granted Faversham a charter and the market still plays an important part in the life of the town today. In the Market Place, which is also the junction of three of the town's oldest streets, stands the **Guildhall** which was built in the 16th century and sits on a pillared arcade.

Although, over the centuries, Faversham market has dealt in a wide range of goods, the town was, for 400 years, the centre of the country's explosives industry and **Chart Gunpowder Mills** is a lasting monument to the industry that thrived here between 1560 and 1934. Dating from the 18th century, and now restored, these mills are the oldest of their kind in the world.

Faversham has over 400 listed buildings and one that is well worth seeking out is the 15th century former inn that is now home to the **Fleur de Lis Heritage Centre**. Here, displays review the last 1,000 years and tell the story of the town's growth and prosperity. Of the numerous artefacts and exhibitions to be seen here one of the more impressive is Abbey Street, a 16th century thoroughfare that is complete and well preserved. At the centre, too, visitors can walk through a doorway that was once used by James II and learn of the story behind the anonymous play *Arden of Feversham*.

PRESTON LEA

Canterbury Road, Faversham, Kent ME13 8XA
Tel: 01795 535266 Fax: 01795 533388
e-mail: preston.lea@which.net website: http://homepages.which.net/~alan.turner10

Built for a local brick manufacturer in the 1890s, **Preston Lea** is a large Gothic style Victorian town house that lies within its own secluded gardens well hidden from the outskirts of Faversham. Guests to this superb bed and breakfast establishment are greeted with tea in the spacious guests' drawing room by owners Alan and Catherine Turner who are always on hand to ensure that guests enjoy their stay to the full. Each of the three individually decorated guest bedrooms, which all have their own

bathroom facilities, overlook the splendid mature gardens that surround the house and which are also available for guests to use.

Breakfast, including vegetarian options, is served in the wood panelled dining room and, whilst no evening meal is served at Preston Lea, there are numerous restaurants and pubs close by. This delightful house, that has been beautifully decorated and furnished throughout to make the most of its Victorian heritage, is a joy to stay at and also one that is ideally situated for exploring the Kent countryside.

THE SHIPWRIGHT'S ARMS

Hollowshore, Faversham,
Kent ME13 7TU
Tel: 01795 590088

Found next to Faversham Creek, **The Shipwright's Arms** is at least 300 years old and, indeed, this lovely old inn does contain traces of a much earlier building that may go back as far as the 13th century. First officially licensed as an inn in 1738, although it probably functioned as such long before this, the Shipwright's Arms has always been popular with sailors and fisherman on the Thames estuary as well as

playing host to pirates and smugglers.

Whilst still welcoming yachtsmen, landlord Derek Cole also plays host to walkers, bird watchers and visitors lucky enough to find this hidden inn. Well known for its excellent real ales and beers, including a special brew called Shipwrecked, this is the perfect place to come to for traditional pub food that, particularly in winter, favours English pies and puddings. The style of the inn's hospitality reflects the wonderful unspoilt interior of this ancient place that, along with the numerous nooks and crannies, has roaring log fires to welcome customers. Not surprisingly, given the history of the inn, there is also a maritime theme here with shipwright's tools and model boats decorated the walls.

Close by lies **Faversham Creek**, a tidal inlet of the River Swale, that is inextricably linked with the main town's prosperity as the Creek acted as Faversham's port. A limb of the Cinque Port of Dover and with a shipbuilding tradition that is so rooted in history that the title of 'The King's Port' is retained as an acknowledgement of the royal gratitude for the provision of navy vessels, Faversham Creek is well worth a visit. Between here and Seasalter, to the east, lies the **South Swale Nature Reserve**, that concentrates on the legacy of natural history of this area. A wide range of wildfowl, including Brent geese, make their home along this stretch of coast.

OSPRINGE
8 miles SW of Whitstable off the A2

This hamlet, just to the southwest of Faversham, was a thriving Roman settlement and around here numerous coins, medallions and household items have been unearthed that suggest that the community was quite sizeable. Various Roman artefacts that have been excavated here can be found, along with Saxon pottery, glass and jewellery and relics from medieval Ospringe, at **Maison Dieu**. Originally founded by Henry III in around 1230, the building served as a combination hospital and hostel for pilgrims on their way to and from Canterbury and, as well as having some features still remaining from the 13th century, the house also displays beamed ceilings from the Tudor era. Along with the relics unearthed in the local area, the museum here also includes some interesting information on Maison Dieu itself.

TEYNHAM
10 miles SW of Whitstable off the A2

In 1533, Henry VIII's fruiterer, Richard Harris, planted England's first cherry tree in the village, along with pippens and golden russett apple trees, and thus established Teynham as the birthplace of English orchards.

3 Canterbury to Sandwich Bay

This ancient land, between the city of Canterbury and the east coast of Kent, has seen invaders come and go, religious houses founded and then dissolved under Henry VIII and the building of great fortresses. Certainly one of the best places to begin any tour of the area is Canterbury itself, the home of the Mother Church of the Anglican Communion, Canterbury Cathedral. The cathedral was founded by St Augustine in the late 6th century, along with an abbey, and both can still be seen today although the cathedral, that still dominates the city's skyline, is actually a Norman structure. The abbey and cathedral, along with St Martin's Church, the oldest parish church in England that is still in constant use, form a fascinating World Heritage Site.

The Beach, Deal

However, its is not just ancient buildings that draw visitors to this very special city. There is much else to see here including the places that were known to the city's several famous literary connections: Geoffrey Chaucer, the Elizabethan playwright and spy Christopher Marlowe, Somerset Maugham and Mary Tourtel, the creator of Rupert Bear.

The land between Canterbury and the coast is characterised by pretty villages, whilst to the south around Barfreston, was the area of the East Kent coalfield. To the north, around Stourmouth, is an area of very fertile land which is the home of market gardens and orchards. Centuries ago, the Wantsum Channel separated the Isle of Thanet from the rest of Kent and, in the 16th and 17th centuries, drainage of the marshland that was created by the silting up of the channel formed the land that is seen today.

This eastern stretch of Kentish coastline supported numerous fishing villages but, with the constant threat of invasion, they became fortified, particularly in 16th century under Henry VIII. Deal Castle remains one of the best surviving examples of Tudor military architecture whilst its contemporary, Walmer Castle, has been turned into an elegant stately house that is the home of the Lord Warden of the Cinque Ports. Set up in the 11th century, the Cinque Ports were a commercial alliance of south coast ports but today the title is chiefly ceremonial and the present Lord Warden is HM Queen Elizabeth, The Queen Mother.

CANTERBURY TO SANDWICH BAY

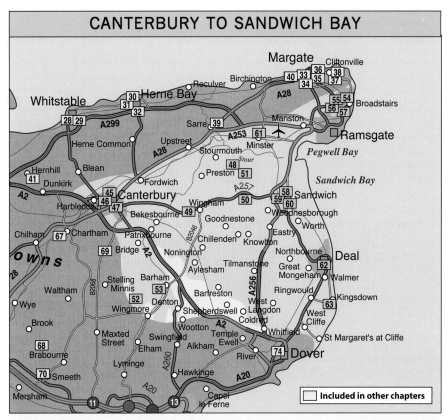

Margate Cliftonville
Birchington 40 33 36 38
34 35 37
Reculver
Whitstable 30 Herne Bay A28
31 55 54 Broadstairs
32 56 57
28 29 A299 Sarre 39 Manston
Herne Common Upstreet A253 61 Ramsgate
A28 Stourmouth Minster Pegwell Bay
Stour
Hernhill Blean 48
41 Dunkirk Fordwich Preston 51 Sandwich Bay
A2 45 Canterbury A257 58 Sandwich
Harbledown 46 Wingham 50 59 60
47 Bekesbourne 49 Goodnestone Woodnesborough
Chilham 67 Chartham Patrixbourne Chillenden Knowlton Worth
69 Bridge Nonington Eastry Northbourne Deal
DOWNS Aylesham Tilmanstone Great 62
Barham Mongeham Walmer
Stelling Ringwould
Waltham Minnis 53 Barfreston 63 Kingsdown
52 Denton West West
Wye Wingmore Shepherdswell Langdon Cliffe
Brook Coldred Whitfield
Wootton A2 St Margaret's at Cliffe
68 Maxted Swingfield Temple
Brabourne Street Elham Alkham Ewell River 74 Dover
Lyminge
70 Smeeth Hawkinge A20
Mersham 11 13 Capel
le Ferne ☐ Included in other chapters

© MAPS IN MINUTES ™ (2000)

PLACES TO STAY, EAT, DRINK AND SHOP

45	Canterbury Cathedral, Canterbury	Cathedral	Page 62
46	The Kent Masonic Library, Canterbury	Museum and library	Page 64
47	The Phoenix, Canterbury	Pub, food & accommodation	Page 64
48	The Way Out Inn, Westmarsh	Pub, restaurant & accommodation	Page 66
49	The Duke William, Ickham	Pub and restaurant	Page 67
50	The Lion Hotel, Ash	Pub with food	Page 68
51	Hawthorn Farm, Ware	Self catering	Page 68
52	Molehills, Bladbean	Bed and breakfast	Page 70
53	Heaseland House, Barham	Bed and breakfast	Page 70
54	Beau's and Brummells, Broadstairs	Café, bar and restaurant	Page 74
55	Ye Olde Crown, Broadstairs	Pub with food	Page 74
56	The Louisa Bay, Broadstairs	Pub with food	Page 75
57	The Queens Hotel, Broadstairs	Hotel	Page 75
58	The Bell Hotel, Sandwich	Hotel and restaurant	Page 76
59	George and Dragon Inn, Sandwich	Pub and restaurant	Page 76
60	Little Cottage Restaurant, Sandwich	Restaurant and tearooms	Page 77
61	The Bell Inn, Minster-in-Thanet	Pub with food	Page 79
62	Hole in the Roof Hotel and Café Bar, Deal	Café, bar, food & accommodation	Page 80
63	Kingsdown Park, Upper Street	Self catering	Page 82

CANTERBURY CATHEDRAL

Cathedral House, 11 the Precincts, Canterbury, Kent CT1 2EH
Tel: 01227 762862 Fax: 01227 865222/865250
e-mail: enquiries@canterbury-cathedral.org website: www.canterbury-cathedral.org

Continuing to dominate the skyline of the city today, Canterbury Cathedral has a tradition of welcoming visitors that goes back to the days of the medieval pilgrimage. It was founded in AD 597 by St

Augustine who was sent to England by Pope Gregory the Great and, as the first archbishop, he made Canterbury his seat (or 'Cathedra'). The earliest part of the present building is the crypt that dates back to around 1100 and that is also the largest of its kind in the country. On top of this was built the quire that had to be replaced in the 12th century after the original construction was destroyed by fire. Gradually, the building was added too and extended over the centuries and, of the more interesting parts, there is the 14th century nave, with its tall columns rising up like trees to meet the delicate vaulted arches, and the late 15th century 'Bell Harry' tower.

The windows in the cathedral are magnificent and all the more so as they have not only survived the ravages of Henry VIII's Dissolution of the Monasteries but also Hitler's bombs that flatted much of the surrounding city. However, the cathedral's library was not so lucky as this was damaged by a German air raid in 1942. Fortunately, the beautiful and historic stained glass at the cathedral had been removed earlier and only the plain, replacement windows were blown out with the force of the blast.

Naturally, there is much to see here, from the medieval tombs of kings and numerous archbishops to splendid architecture and the guided tours provide not only information about the building but

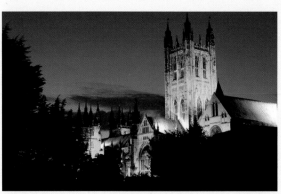

also of those people who have been associated with it through the centuries. However, it is as the scene of the murder of Archbishop Thomas à Becket that the building is best known. Becket was killed on a December evening in the northwest transept by the knights of Henry II who misunderstood the king's request to be ridden of his archbishop. A penitent Henry, full of remorse for the death of his former friend, later came here on a pilgrimage. Unfortunately, Becket's tomb, that is said to have been covered in gold and jewels, was destroyed in 1538 by the agents of Henry VIII. However, from the time of his death, in 1170, Canterbury Cathedral has been one of the most famous places of pilgrimage in Europe and it continues to be so today. Standing in spacious precincts surrounded by the remains of a monastery, the cathedral, along with St Martin's Church and St Augustine's Abbey, form a World Heritage Site.

CANTERBURY

England's most famous cathedral city, and also one of the loveliest, Canterbury lies in one of the most attractive areas of rural Kent. It was here, in AD 597, that St Augustine founded an abbey, soon after his arrival from Rome, and it proved to be the roots of Christianity in England. Lying just outside the city walls, **St Augustine's Abbey** is now in ruins but there is an excellent museum and information centre here with exhibits on display that have been excavated from the site. Before St Augustine had finished the monastery, he worshipped at **St Martin's Church**, England's oldest parish church, that was named after the Bishop of Tours, France. The building is believed to date back to Roman times and it is still in constant use.

Canterbury Cathedral

However, both these fine buildings are overshadowed by the Mother Church of the Anglican Communion, **Canterbury Cathedral**, that still dominates the city today (see panel opposite) . One of the best examples of ecclesiastical architecture in the country and England's first cathedral, it was founded, in 597, by St Augustine and it was here that he converted numerous Saxons to Christianity before his death some seven years later. Best known as the scene of the murder of Archbishop Thomas à Becket in the 12th century, Canterbury Cathedral has been one of Europe's most important places of pilgrimage ever since and particularly so during the Middle Ages. Today, the Archbishop of Canterbury is the Primate of All England, attends royal functions and sits in the House of Lords and the present incumbent, Dr George Carey, is the 103rd archbishop.

By the time that Geoffrey Chaucer was writing his *Canterbury Tales*, some two centuries after the death of Thomas à Becket in 1170, Canterbury had become a very popular place of pilgrimage that was second only to Rome and Jerusalem. Many of the pilgrims set out, on foot or by horse, from London, as did Chaucer himself, and, in many cases, the journey seems to have been more of a social event than an act of penance. As well as making the journey at least once himself, as the King's messenger, Chaucer also passed through Canterbury on numerous occasions on his way to the Continent. At the **Canterbury Tales Visitor Attraction** visitors are taken back to the 14th century and invited to embark on the same journey of pilgrimage that was undertaken by the characters in Chaucer's great poem. As they were making the journey, the Knight, the Miller, the Pardoner and the Wife of Bath, along with the other travellers, told tales to keep themselves amused. From the animated farmyard tale of a cock, a hen and a wily old fox to stories of love, rivalry and chivalry, the colourful tales are brought very much to life at this popular attraction.

Whilst Canterbury is certainly dominated by its great cathedral there is much more to the city than first appearances might suggest. The capital of the Iron Age kingdom, Cantii (a name that lives on in the city and in the county name of Kent), the Romans also settled here for a time and, at the **Roman Museum**, there is a fine display of unearthed remains from Dunrovernum Cantiacorum (the Roman name for Canterbury). This underground museum centres on the remains of a Roman town house and, along with the fine mosaic floors, there are also reconstructions of other Roman buildings, a gallery of household objects that were excavated in

THE KENT MASONIC LIBRARY AND MUSEUM

St Peter's Place, Canterbury, Kent CT1 2DA
Tel: 01227 785625

This ancient city is home to a particularly unusual museum - **The Kent Masonic Library and Museum** - where the history of freemasonry, from its begins in the county through to the present day are explored. With special emphasis on East and West Kent, the museum has numerous exhibits that include some fine paintings, glassware and porcelain and the Cornwallis collection of documents and presentation items. There is also a vast collection of books covering all aspects of freemasonry and, of course, a display of Masonic regalia. The museum has limited opening times during the week and guided tours with the curator can be arranged.

THE PHOENIX

67 Old Dover Road, Canterbury, Kent CT1 3DB
Tel: 01227 464220

Conveniently located on the south side of Canterbury is **The Phoenix**, a welcoming and inviting inn that is within with handy walking distance of the city centre and the County Cricket ground. Originally known as the Bridge House Tavern, the inn acquired its present name - quite understandably - when it was rebuilt after a serious fire in 1962.

Today's landlords, Keith and Linda Barker, are a local couple and they were customers here until taking over the license in February 2000. Very well placed to understand exactly the requirements of their regulars, Keith, Linda and their West Highland Terrier, Benji, have created a warm and relaxed atmosphere where visitors are sure to feel at home.

As well as serving a good selection of drinks from the bar, including four real ales, The Phoenix also offers a menu of traditional pub food. In particular, firm favourites here are the liver and bacon, the steam meat pudding, the Kentish speciality Gypsy Tart and the Sunday roast lunches for which booking is advisable. Visitors to the area will be interested to hear that Keith and Linda also provide comfortable bed and breakfast accommodation in a choice of three guest bedrooms.

The Weavers House, Canterbury

and around this site and some reproduction artefacts that visitors can handle. Another aspect of life in Kent can be discovered at **The Kent Masonic Library and Museum** where the history of freemasonry over the last 300 years is explored. The vast collections found here cover many aspects of masonic life and visitors can, in particular, see numerous pieces of Masonic regalia and a huge library of books (see panel opposite).

Meanwhile, housed in the former Poor Priests' Hospital, that has some fine medieval interiors, is the **Canterbury Heritage Museum** that presents a full history of the city over the last 2,000 years. From the time of the Roman occupation through to Canterbury in World War II, this museum has a great wealth of treasures and award winning displays that are sure to excite and

interest the whole family. Among the various displays here can be found memorabilia relating to Mary Tourtel, the creator of Rupert Bear, who was born in Canterbury in 1874.

In fact, Canterbury has had a surprisingly large number of connections with the literary world down the ages as, along with Mary Tourtel and, of course, Chaucer, Somerset Maugham went to King's School in the city in the 1890s as did the Elizabethan dramatist Christopher Marlowe centuries earlier. A contemporary of Shakespeare's and the author of *Dr Faustus* and *Edward II*, Marlowe, the son of a shoemaker, was born in 1564 in George Street, Canterbury and later went on to Benet (now Corpus Christi) College Cambridge. As a friend of Sir Francis Walsingham, Elizabeth I's Secretary of State, Marlowe supplemented his literary career by taking an active role as a spy. At only 29 years of age, he was stabbed to death in Deptford following what is officially referred to as a tavern brawl but what was more likely to have been a deliberately planned assassination. He is buried at the church of St Nicholas and the church records simply state: "Christopher Marlowe, slain by ffrancis Archer 1 June 1593." Canterbury's main theatrical venue, the **Marlowe Theatre**, is named after this famous son and, along with the **Gulbenkian Theatre** at the University of Kent, it plays host to the annual **Canterbury Festival** that presents a varied programme of performing arts.

AROUND CANTERBURY

FORDWICH
2½ miles NE of Canterbury off the A28

This village was once a busy port, serving all of Canterbury's trade, on the River Stour that was tidal to this point. As the

THE WAY OUT INN

Westmarsh, near Ash, Canterbury, Kent CT3 2LP
Tel: 01304 812899 Fax: 01304 813181
e-mail: Mail@TheWayOutInn.com website: www.TheWayOutInn.com

Found tucked away amongst the orchards of the small village of Westmarsh, yet close to many of the area's historical attractions such as Canterbury cathedral and the castles at Dover and Walmer, **The Way Out Inn** is a place much loved by the locals that is well worth seeking out. A quiet country

haven, from which there are several short and appealing countryside walks as well as part of the Saxon Shore Way Walk, those finding themselves at the inn can be certain of a warm welcome and some excellent hospitality.

Although the present building only dates back to 1896, The Way Out Inn was built on the site of the former Elizabethan inn - which was burnt to the ground in 1895 - and this in turn was constructed on the site of a medieval farm.

Today's owners, Hazel and Cardy Cruttwell, have been here since the mid 1980s and, whilst they are both experienced and congenial hosts, they were also born and bred in Kent and so have an excellent understanding of the area as well as their regular customers. The inn's interior has a bright and traditional atmosphere that is enhanced by the well chosen furnishings and decoration and the prints of local scenes hanging from the walls. A friendly and comfortable free house, from the bar Hazel and Cardy serve a wide range of drinks including at least three real ales, ciders and stouts. The high standard of the food that is served here at both lunchtime and in the evening (in the restaurant and in the bar) has helped to make this a popular and successful inn and, with both Hazel and Cardy taking a hand in kitchen, the delicious meals are very much home-cooked. Pies are a speciality here, as is the Sunday roast lunch and, to avoid disappointment, it is always advisable to book at weekends.

However, superb food and drink is not all that is on offer here as, outside, there is a large, secluded beer garden, complete with children's play area, a giant wooden Wendy House and two Bat and Trap pitches. In a separate building from the inn, that was built in 1999, Hazel and Cardy also provide wonderful accommodation that reaches the same high standards as the rest of their delightful establishment. Whilst most of the accommodation is let on a bed and breakfast basis, there is also a self-contained flat that is ideal for friends or a family looking to spend time in this wonderful location.

river silted up and commercial vessels became larger, Fordwich was robbed of its major economic activity and the once prosperous town became a quiet and peaceful backwater. However, remnants of the bustling trade that was carried out here remain and the village is home to one of the smallest **Town Hall's** in the county, this one having been built in Tudor times.

PRESTON
7 miles NE of Canterbury off the A28

Listed in the Domesday Book as Prestetune, which means 'priest's farmstead or manor', the village church of St Mildred had, up until the early 18th century, suffered a period of decline and records show that animals were allowed to graze in the graveyard and that the church services were conducted improperly if they were conducted at all.

However, some sort of order was returned to the parish when, in 1711, a house was left to the local church for use as a vicarage on condition that two services were held at the church each Sunday.

STOURMOUTH
7½ miles NE of Canterbury off the A28

As the village is several miles from the sea, its name seems to make little sense but, centuries ago, this is where the River Stour fed into the **Wantsum Channel**, the stretch of water that separates the Isle of Thanet from the rest of Kent. In fact, such was the depth of the channel that, in AD 885, it was the site of a sea battle between King Alfred and Danish raiders who became trapped in the channel whilst attempting to attack and capture Rochester.

The Wantsum Channel gradually silted up over the years and, in the 16th and

THE DUKE WILLIAM

The Street, Ickham, near Littlebourne, Canterbury, Kent CT3 1QP
Tel: 01227 721308 Fax: 01227 722042
e-mail: stuartmcneill@ukgateway.net

Originally built in 1611 and first becoming an inn in 1790, **The Duke William** is a charming and attractive old building that is made all the more eyecatching by the mass of colourful hanging baskets, tubs and window boxes that adorn its frontage. The interior of the inn is equally inviting and here, in these traditional English pub surroundings, customers will find a warm and friendly atmosphere, a roaring fire in winter and caricatures of local villagers hanging on the walls.

This is very much a family run establishment and Alistair and Carol McNeill have been here since 1982 and they are now ably helped by their son Stuart. Well known for their excellent selection of real ales - many of which come of independent breweries - The Duke William is highly regarded for its food and it features in all the good guides. Alistair trained and worked at Quaglinos in London and, naturally, he oversees the preparation of the splendid à la carte menu that offers a range of international dishes that are all freshly cooked to order. An authorised member

for real food, dining at The Duke William is certainly an experience to savour.

17th centuries, the resultant marshes were drained by Flemish refugees. Still criss-crossed by a network of drainage ditches today, this land remains very fertile and it is now home to market gardens, fruit farms and hops.

WINGHAM
6 miles E of Canterbury on the A257

On either side of the long tree-lined High Street, that runs through this large village, there are some fine and historic buildings, some of which date back to the reign of Henry VIII. There is an interesting story

THE LION HOTEL

60 The Street, Ash, Canterbury, Kent CT3 2EW
Tel: 01304 813141

Situated beside the main Canterbury to Sandwich road, in the heart of the village of Ash, **The Lion Hotel** is a striking old building that dates back to 1534. The splendid interior of this wonderful ancient inn is as full of character and charm as the outside would suggest and, taking pride of place in the bar, is the log burning stove. The low beamed ceilings and wood panelled walls also add to the cosy environment of this inn which is also well known for its friendly and welcoming atmosphere. Owners, Stephanie and Graham not only take great pride in offering an excellent range of drinks from the bar, including several real ales, but they also cook and the menu here is a mouth-watering list of dishes. Everything is home-made and among the tempting list are the house specialities - steak and kidney pie, liver and onions and Shepherd's pie. A very popular inn with those living in the area, Stephanie and Graham also extend a warm welcome to visitors and children who not only come here to enjoy the superb food, drink and atmosphere but also to enjoy the occasional live entertainment this hospitable couple lay on. There is a large family garden at the rear and parking nearby.

HAWTHORN FARM

Corner Drove, Ware, near Ash, Kent CT3 2LU
Tel: 01304 813560 Fax: 01304 812482 e-mail: info@hawthornfarm.co.uk
website: www.hawthornfarm.co.uk

Ideally located for touring eastern Kent or taking a day trip across the Channel to France, **Hawthorn Farm** lies in a quiet and peaceful part of the Kentish countryside. Surrounded by beautiful landscaped gardens, which play host to a wide variety of birds and wildlife and where owls, kingfishers and woodpeckers have been sighted, Hawthorn Farm comprises four attractive holiday cottages, a splendid barn conversion farmhouse, stables and a playing field.

Owners, John and Lindsey Baker, who live at the farmhouse, have been here since August 1999 and they have provided the

perfect place for families and friends to enjoy a relaxed and carefree holiday in comfort. Each of the four cottages have been converted from old farm buildings and they each have their own garden where guests can take full advantage of the summer evening sunshine. Fully equipped to a high standard and, as well as kitchen and homely living area, there are two charming bedrooms and a bathroom that make each of the cottages ideal for families. The large playing field is perfect for children's ball games and well behaved dogs can also join in the family fun here. Though self contained and in the heart of rural Kent, the local pub, The Way Out Inn, is just a short stroll away.

Once you have enjoyed the farm as a holiday location, you are likely to be tempted to return for one of the many NLP training events held throughout the year.

surrounding the wooden arcade of the **Norman parish church**. By the 16th century the building had fallen into a state of acute disrepair and George Ffoggarde, a local brewer, obtained a licence to raise funds for the church's repair. However, Ffoggarde embezzled all the £244 that he had collected and so the intended stone arcade which was going to have been a feature of the repairs was replaced with a wooden one that was considerably cheaper. Whilst there is no particular tradition of defrauding in Wingham, the village did become renowned for rebellion as the villagers were not only active in the Peasants' Revolt of 1381 and other popular protests but they also took part in the Swing Riots of 1830 for which several inhabitants were transported to Australia.

Just to the northeast of the village lies **Wingham Bird Park** which aims to provide safe and secure habitats for many species of bird that are threatened in the wild. Among the many birds here visitors can see waterfowl, parrots, owls and emu whilst, in the Orchard Aviary, numerous smaller birds live alongside a range of furry mammals. Children, in particular, will enjoy the Pet Village where they can mingle with the animals and the Landscaped Lake where they can feed the ducks. For others there is the special observation shelter, along with a gift shop, tea room and adventure playground.

BEKESBOURNE
3 miles SE of Canterbury off the A2

Just to the north of the village and set within 70 acres of beautiful and ancient parkland, lies **Howletts Wild Animal Park** which was created by John Aspinall and that is dedicated to the preservation of rare and endangered animals. Here, visitors can see the largest family groups of gorillas and the biggest breeding herd

of African elephants kept in captivity, certainly, within Europe if not the world. Other families of rare monkeys can be seen at the park along with both Indian and Siberian tigers, other large cats and many more endangered animals.

PATRIXBOURNE
3 miles SE of Canterbury off the A2

This handsome village, with a range of houses dating largely from the 17th and 18th centuries, also has newer dwellings that, when they were built in the 19th century, were carefully constructed in the Tudor style. The admirable results would certainly please Prince Charles and they blend harmoniously with the existing buildings. Meanwhile, the village church dates back to Norman times and it has some wonderful carvings including, in particular, the priest's door with a disfigured saint's head above.

AYLESHAM
6½ miles SE of Canterbury off the B2046

Following World War I, the eminent town planner, Professor Abercrombie, set out an ambitious scheme for a new town here that was to provide housing for 15,000 people. When development began in the 1920s, the plans were scaled down and the village provided dwellings for miners and their families who worked in the East Kent coalfield and, in particular, nearby Snowdown Colliery which closed in 1987.

GOODNESTONE
7 miles SE of Canterbury off the B2046

Close to the village lies Goodnestone Park, an estate that was originally owned by Brook Bridges, who held an important post in the Treasury during the reign of Charles II. In the 18th century, Jane Austen was a frequent visit to the house as her brother married Bridges' daughter and, during World War II, the house and

MOLEHILLS

Bladbean, Canterbury,
Kent CT4 6LU
Tel: 01303 840051
Mobile: 07808 639942
e-mail:
molehills84@hotmail.com

Dating from the 1920s and found in a quiet and spacious garden, **Molehills** was originally built for the minister of the Methodist chapel that lies adjacent to the property and that is now, itself, a private house. This pretty establishment, in the beautiful Elham Valley, is the home of Min and Dick Barham who offer friendly bed and breakfast accommodation to anyone lucky enough to find this secluded hamlet. There are two en suite guest bedrooms that are, like the rest of the house, tastefully furnished and decorated and guests at Molehills also have their own dining room, sitting room and conservatory.

A former chemistry teacher at Kings in Canterbury, Dick has now turned his hand to growing organic vegetables in the garden. Guests will find that at breakfast and for the evening meal, that can be arranged, only his home-grown vegetables and fruit are used, when in season, and guests can also wander the garden and see his hard work.

HEASELAND HOUSE

Barham, near Canterbury,
Kent CT4 6LA
Tel: 01227 831643

Found in a peaceful, rural location between Canterbury and Dover and close to Lydden motor racing circuit, **Heaseland House** is a beautiful 18th century farmhouse that is now the home of Valerie and Thomas Denne and their black Labrador Flora.

The couple, who were both born in Kent, offer superb bed and breakfast accommodation from their lovely house in a choice of three delightful guest rooms. Each has been tastefully furnished and decorated with comfort in mind and, with views out over the large, well tendered garden, anyone staying here is sure to have a relaxing night's sleep. A home-cooked breakfast is served in the elegant surroundings of the dining room and special diets, such as vegetarian, can be catered for.

There is also a large guest lounge here that, like the rest of the house, is not only well decorated but furnished with interesting antique furniture. The perfect place to rest at the end of the day, an open fire adds an extra glow on colder evenings.

park was requisitioned by the army and used as a tank repair depot. The estate is now in the ownership of Lord and Lady FitzWalter and **Goodnestone Park Gardens** are considered some of the best in the southeast of England. The formal gardens around the house contain several old specimen trees along with a walled garden that still has some of the original 17th century walls. New planting continues here all the time and beyond the formal garden areas lie mature woodlands with a 1920s rockery and pond.

NONINGTON
7 miles SE of Canterbury off the B2046

For many years there were several private estates, with grand and imposing houses, situated close to this village and one, **Fredville Park**, remains to the south of Nonington. Although the superb Georgian house that lay at the centre of this estate was burnt to the ground in 1939, the park is still renowned for its fine oak trees and, in particular, the **Fredville Oak** that is several hundred years old and has a circumference of 36 feet.

CHILLENDEN
8 miles SE of Canterbury off the B2046

Found in a prominent position, just outside this village, is **Chillenden Windmill**, one of the last 'open trestle' post windmills to be built in England and one of the last surviving such mills in Kent. It was built in 1868 for Brigadier Speed, who lived at Knowlton Court, although this exposed site has supported windmills for over 500 years. Restored recently and with a complete outward appearance, the mill contains some of the old machinery and it is open to the public on occasional days throughout the year.

KNOWLTON
8½ miles SE of Canterbury off the A256

The main street through this tiny hamlet leads to **Knowlton Court** that, down the years, has been the home of several military and naval men. The Royalist commander, Sir Thomas Peyton lived here around the time of the Civil War whilst, later, it was the home of Admiral Sir John Narborough. In 1707, Sir John's two sons were drowned off the Isles of Scilly following a naval disaster when navigational error caused the English fleet to be wrecked at night. A tomb in **Knowlton Church**, designed by Grinling Gibbons, illustrates the scene.

BARFRESTON
8½ miles SE of Canterbury off the A2

This pretty village lies in the heart of farming land, just to the north of Lyminge Forest, although, up until World War II much of the land in this immediate area was taken over by collieries. Barfreston's small **Norman church**, that dates from the 11th and 12th centuries, is remarkable for its detailed stone carvings the best examples of which can be seen around the east door. Representing an array of creatures, scenes from medieval life and religious symbols, an explanatory booklet on these delightful images can be obtained from the nearby public house. There is another curious feature to this church - the church bell can be found attached to a yew tree in the churchyard.

SHEPHERDSWELL
9 miles SE of Canterbury off the A2

This old village, which is sometimes referred to as Sibertswold, grew rapidly after 1861 when the London to Dover railway opened and, again, when housing was built here for the miners working at the nearby Tilmanstone Colliery. In 1911, a junction was established for the East Kent Light Railway, that served the colliery and, whilst the last passenger service ran in 1948, the railway continued its commercial operations until the colliery closed in 1987. Today, the **East Kent Railway** is open once again and it carries passengers for pleasure from the village's charming station, to the nearby village of Eythorne, on restored trains. Those visiting the railway will find that there is also a museum of railway memorabilia, a buffet, a gift shop and a miniature railway to add to their enjoyment.

COLDRED
10 miles SE of Canterbury off the A2

Next to the parish church of St Pancras lies a farm that was originally a manor house owned by Bishop Odo of Bayeux, half-brother to William the Conqueror. In fact, both the church and the farm stand on a site that was a fortified Saxon camp of the 8th century and a few remains can still be seen. Archaeological excavations in this ancient village have revealed not only finds from Saxon times but also evidence of earlier, Roman, occupation. More recently, the village pond was used for witch trails and, in the 1640s, it was recorded that Nell Garlige, an old woman of the parish, was tied up and thrown into the pond where, presumably, she drowned.

HARBLEDOWN
1 mile NW of Canterbury off the A2

This village was, for many pilgrims, their last stopping place before Canterbury and, so legend has it, the village well was called Black Prince's Well as the prince believed the waters to have healing properties. Despite drinking a flask of the water each day, the prince died in 1376, probably of syphilis that he contracted in Spain.

BLEAN
2½ miles NW of Canterbury on the A290

Close to the village lies **Druidstone Wildlife Park** where visitors can see a wide variety of animals and birds in a peaceful country setting. Along with the native species here, some of which are now rare, such as otters and owls, the park is also home to more exotic creatures including Rhea, mara, wallabies and parrots. Younger children can make friends with the farmyard animals whilst there are walks through woodland where the park's herd of deer can be observed. Many of the animals and birds living here have been rescued whilst others play an important part in captive breeding programmes. Meanwhile, the surroundings of the park also provide interest, right throughout the year, from spring flowers to autumn fungi and winter buds.

RAMSGATE

For centuries, Ramsgate was a small fishing village until, in 1749, a harbour was built here and the town began to grow. After George IV landed here in 1822, (the **obelisk** on the East Pier commemorates this historic event) the town adopted the title of 'Royal Harbour' and, by the end of the 19th century, its fishing fleet had grown to make this the largest port on the south coast of England. However, at the beginning of World War I, the fishing industry began to decline and, with a seemingly uncertain future, Ramsgate enjoyed a brief moment of national glory when, in 1940, over 40,000 British troops, evacuated from the Dunkirk beaches by an armada of small boats and vessels, landed here. The parish church of St George commemorates this important episode in Ramsgate's and

England's history with a special stained glass window.

Still dominated by its harbour and shipping, the town is also home to the **Ramsgate Motor Museum** where visitors are offered a trip down memory lane and a journey back to the days of stylish motoring. Founded in 1982 and dedicated to the golden ages of motoring, the many cars, motorcycles and bicycles on display here are set out in scenes that depict the past and cards record the world history of the year each vehicle was made.

Broadstairs Beach

Just to the south of Ramsgate lies **Pegwell Bay** that is, traditionally, said to have been the landing place of Hengist and Horsa who led the successful Jutish invasion of Kent in AD 449. The badge of Kent today has on it a prancing white horse, the same image under which these Jutish warriors fought.

AROUND RAMSGATE

BROADSTAIRS
2 miles N of Ramsgate on the A255

This family seaside resort, that grew as an amalgamation of St Peter's inland and Broadstairs and Reading on the coast, still retains its village atmosphere though it is best known for its associations with Charles Dickens. Those coming in search of **Bleak House** will find it high up on the cliffs at the northern end of the town, overlooking the popular beach at Viking Bay, and the town retains its links with the great Victorian novelist by holding an annual Charles Dickens Festival.

Other famous people associated with the town include the politician Sir Edward Heath, who was born here in 1916, and another famous sailor, Sir Alec Rose, who lived in Broadstairs for many years. Writers too seem to have found inspiration along this stretch of coast as both Frank Richards, creator of Billy Bunter, and John Buchan, author of *The Thirty-Nine Steps* spy thriller, lived here. Buchan wrote the story at a house called St Cuby, on Cliff Promenade and the staircase that gave him the idea for the title stands opposite the house. Actually of 78 steps, this was halved by Buchan to provide a catchier title.

Bleak House, Broadstairs

BEAU'S AND BRUMMELLS

8 Charlotte Street, Broadstairs,
Kent CT10 1LR
Tel: 01843 862771 Fax: 01843 869351

Tucked away behind the town's main street lies **Beau's and Brummells** a stylish and attractive premises that is Beau's Café Bar during the day and Brummells Restaurant in the evening. During the day in this versatile Restaurant/Café Bar, not only can you just sit and drink, but also have the chance of a 'lite bite' or a three course meal. On Sunday a 2 or 3 course Roast Lunch with a selection of meats, fish and imaginative vegetarian choices, is available.

In the evening, the restaurant tranforms into Brummell's, a first class London style eating house under the direction of the proprietor Richard Tebbutt-Ford whose expertise was garnered from his work at the Ritz Hotel London, Boodles Gentleman's Club St James', Buckingham Palace, Windsor Castle, as well as a time at the Chateau Tilques, St Omer.

The menu offers a sophisticated and imaginative range of dishes which include fish and unusual meats such as ostrich. The vegetarian selection is varied and the wine list reflects the high quality of the food. Together with the surroundings, this makes an ideal for a tête-à-tête or a party.

YE OLDE CROWN

23 High Street, Broadstairs, Kent CT10 1LP
Tel: 01843 861747

Beginning life as three fishermen's cottages, **Ye Olde Crown** is a distinctive inn that lies in the heart of the town centre. A busy and popular inn, landlords, Stephen and Emma King, have been here since the spring of 1999 and, in that short time, they have certainly made this one of the liveliest places in Broadstairs.

Both the main bar, and the smaller back bar, offer customers plenty of comfortable seating and, whilst little remains of the building's original features, there are some interesting photographs and pictures on the walls. The perfect place to stop and relax whilst visiting the town, there are always three real ales on tap at the bar along with all the usual beers, lagers and spirits.

Meanwhile, anyone venturing here on a Sunday

afternoon will also find that the regular live music session in full swing. Food, at both lunchtime and in the evening, will be available at Ye Olde Crown from the summer of 2001.

THE LOUISA BAY

Grand Mansions, Queens Gardens, Broadstairs,
Kent CT10 1QE
Tel: 01843 861201

Found in a prime location in Broadstairs, **The Louisa Bay** is an interesting and popular public house that offers its customers the very best in both food and drink. The inn occupies the ground floor of Grand Mansions, an impressive building that was constructed in 1882 as the Grand Hotel. One of the 'most charmingly situated in the Isle of Thanet', this hotel had its main entrance at street level but also an entrance from Louisa Gap and its grounds covered a large area of the cliff tops. After being taken over the army during World War II the hotel was converted into private apartments, although the swimming pool and ball room continued to be used until the 1970s.

Although some of the grandeur of this large Victorian hotel has gone, its superb position, overlooking the sea from the cliff tops has certainly not been lost. Owned since the mid 1980s by Adrian and Vennessa Houson-Ball, The Louisa Bay is managed by Eric Pearson and under his guidance this has become a pub renowned for its good food, drink and entertainment. In the traditional beamed ceiling surrounding the bar, customers can enjoy a wide range of drinks, including real ales, draught lagers and draught ciders, and there is also a tempting menu of home-cooked dishes served at both lunchtime and in the evening. Children are welcome here, until mid evening, and they have their own purpose built padded play area to keep them amused. A resident DJ provides live entertainment on Friday and Saturday evenings and those interested in sport will find that The Louisa Bay provides ample opportunity to keep up to date as they have several televisions devoted to sport.

THE QUEENS HOTEL

31 Queens Road, Broadstairs, Kent CT10 1PG
Tel: 01843 861727 Fax: 01843 600993
e-mail: enquiries@queenshotel.org website: www.queenshotel.org

Found in the heart of Broadstairs, **The Queens Hotel** dates from the late Victorian and early Edwardian eras and it is ideally placed for both the town's amenities and popular Viking Bay. Today, however, this is a small and friendly family hotel that is owned and personally run by Andy and Sharon Crook.

There are nine guest rooms, most of which are en suite, and as well as being comfortably furnished

and pleasantly decorated they also vary in size to provide accommodation in both double and single rooms. As the hotel is licensed, guests can enjoy a drink and some good conversation in the attractive lounge bar before moving through to the spacious and airy dining room and their home-cooked evening meal. Breakfast too is served in these attractive surroundings.

This is very much a family run hotel, where close attention is paid to ensuring guests have a relaxed and enjoyable stay.

THE BELL HOTEL

The Quay, Sandwich, Kent CT13 9EF
Tel: 01304 613388 Fax: 01304 615308
e-mail hotel@princes-leisure.co.uk
website www.princes-leisure.co.uk

The Bell Hotel can be found overlooking the historic
quay in the heart of the ancient port of Sandwich and
offers hospitality and refreshment to travellers and
visitors to the town. The hotel has stood on the present
site since the early 17th century although an earlier
Bell Inn is believed to have existed as far back as the
14th century.

Renowned for its warm welcome this small hotel prides itself on providing a high level of personal
service to ensure that every stay is a memorable one. There are 33 spacious bedrooms, which are
individually designed and furnished, each offering en-suite facilities and enjoying views over the
river or the rooftops of the town. The elegant Honfleur Restaurant can seat up to 50 diners and offers
a superb choice of fine English and French cuisine created by the resident chef, with the selections
being available from the fixed price Plat du Jour or the A La Carte menus. The restaurant is open to

non-residents and advance reservations are recommended. Drinks,
before or after your meal, can be enjoyed in either the cosy Cocktail
Bar or the more contemporary setting of Magnum's Wine Bar.

Owned by the same company is the nearby Princes Golf Course
which offers 27 championship holes and enjoys a reputation as one
of the best modern links courses. Prince's has hosted a number of
major Championships as well as its own well known amateur events.
Special golfing breaks are offered at The Bell Hotel throughout the
year.

GEORGE AND DRAGON INN

24 Fisher Street, Sandwich,
Kent CT13 9EJ
Tel: 01304 613106
Fax: 01304 621137

The award winning **George and
Dragon** is one of Sandwich's several
historic buildings and it dates from
1446 when it was built as a house.
Gaining a licence to sell drink in
1552, the ale house took the name
George and Dragon in 1615 and,
since then, it has never closed.
During the Napoleonic Wars in the
early 19th century, the inn was used
as a recruitment centre which lead
to it, for a while, having the
nickname - 'The Recruiting House'.

Today, this wonderful building
is a superb inn that, whilst retaining many of its old features, has a light and airy feel that is due to the
clever mix of antiquity and modern furniture and decoration. Owners, Liz and Randolph Tillings
have been here since 1996 and, as well as the magnificent environment they have created, they have
also turned the George and Dragon into a lovely place that is highly regarded for its food. Specialising
in locally caught fish, the menus here are both interesting and imaginative that offer a tantalising
choice that would put many larger restaurants to shame. An extensive wine list complements the
dishes served here and, of course, there is the bar. The friendly, smartly dressed professional staff all
help to ensure that this is a dining experience worth savouring.

Church Street, Sandwich

SANDWICH
5½ miles SW of Ramsgate off the A256

Though not a big town, Sandwich has its origins in Saxon times when a town was established here at the mouth of the River Stour. Since those days, the river has silted up and the town now stands a couple of miles from the coast but its maritime history still lives on here. One of the original Cinque ports, hard though it might be to believe today, Sandwich was one of the country's most important naval bases although, by the 15th century this period of its history was over as the harbour was no longer viable. Instead,

the town turned to cloth manufacturing as its economic mainstay and, with the help of Flemish refugees, the town once again prospered. Today, however, this industry has all but ceased and Sandwich has become a very pleasant and peaceful place that is renowned for its championship golf course, Royal St George's.

Sandwich does have plenty to offer the visitor and certainly one of the best places to begin exploration is the **Sandwich Museum**. Telling the story of the town from early medieval times onwards, there are numerous artefacts here that date from as far back as the 13th century. Built in 1576, though it has been modified during the 20th century, the **Guildhall** can be toured and, within its walls, are some fascinating historic items including the Moot Horn that was used as far back as the 12th century to summon the people of the town to hear important announcements. The Horn is still used today to announce the death of the monarch and the accession of their

LITTLE COTTAGE TEA ROOMS & RESTAURANT
The Quay, Sandwich, Kent CT13 9EN
Tel: 10304 614387

Overlooking the River Stour and situated in the ancient area of Sandwich, the **Little Cottage Restaurant and Tea Rooms** is a delightful place that is housed in a building which dates back to the reign of Henry VIII and is said to be haunted. During its long history this interesting building has been many things, including a warehouse, a house of ill-repute and part of a theatre, but today it is a wonderful cosy and intimate tea rooms that has a fine local reputation. Owned and personally run by Denise Brown, with the help of Nicki Batchelor and daughter-in-law Vicki, the Little Cottage Restaurant and Tea Rooms is a popular place where customers can not only be sure of a warm welcome but also some delicious home-cooked food. The extensive menu ranges from freshly filled sandwiches and breakfast (available till 11.00), to luscious home-made cakes and a Sunday roast lunch - there is also a good selection of vegetarian dishes. However, what makes the Little Cottage really special is the attention to detail: there are colouring books for the children, free coffee refills and service is always with a smile.

successor. Another fascinating item is the Hog Mace, which, as the name implies, was used to round up straying animals after the Goose Bell had been rung and, all such animals, not repossessed by their owners on payment of a fine, were passed on to the Brothers and Sisters of St John's Hospital.

Elsewhere in Sandwich, visitors can see the **Barbican Gate**, a turreted 16th century gatehouse that guards the northern entrance into the town, and **St Bartholomew's Hospital**, which was founded in the 12th century and consists of a quadrangle of almshouses grouped around an old chapel.

Found just over a mile northwest of the town is **Richborough Roman Fort** that is believed to date from AD 43. These impressive ruins of a fort and supporting township include the massive foundations of a triumphal arch that stood some 80 feet high. The extensive fortifications, which still dominate the surrounding flat land, were designed to repel Saxon invaders in the 3rd to 5th centuries and, at one time, this was the most important Roman military base in Britain. The museum here gives a real insight into life during the heyday of this busy Roman town.

WORTH
6 miles SW of Ramsgate off the A258

The pond in the centre of this pretty village was once part of a navigable creek that lead out to the sea but, over the centuries, as with much of this coastal strip, the waters have silted up. There are several buildings in Worth that have distinctive Dutch architectural features and these were constructed, in the 17th century, by Flemish and Huguenot refugees who fled from the Continent to escape persecution.

WOODNESBOROUGH
7 miles SW of Ramsgate off the A256

In the early 8th century the Battle of Wodnesbeorh took place here between the Saxon and the West Mercians and, so legend has it, the large mound on which the village is built is actually the burial heap of those who died in the battle. Death certainly seems to have been a feature of ancient Woodnesborough as this is also believed to be the burial place of Vortimer, King of the Saxons, who died in AD 457.

MANSTON
2 miles W of Ramsgate on the B2050

This quiet village, that is surrounded by rich farmland that supports intensive market gardening, was, during World War II home to one of the country's major airfields. Featuring heavily in the Battle of Britain, RAF Manston was the closest airfield to the enemy coast and, as a consequence, it bore the brunt of the early Luftwaffe air attacks. The **Spitfire and Hurricane Memorial Building**, where the main attractions are the two aircraft themselves, provides visitors with an opportunity to gain an understanding of just what life was like for the pilots and other staff stationed at the airfield in the 1940s. Photographs and other memorabilia are on sale here whilst there is a cafeteria with fine views out across the airfield.

MINSTER
4½ miles W of Ramsgate off the A299

It is likely that there were settlements in the area around this village, that overlooks Minster Marshes, well before the invasion of the Romans and it is generally accepted that, later, the Isle of Thanet was the first landing place for invading Saxons. Among the many old buildings in the village, some of which date back to the Middle Ages, there is, in particular, the **Old House** that was built in 1350 and the **Oak House** that is almost as old. One of the country's first nunneries was established at Minster in the 7th century, on land granted to Princess Ermenburga, who is usually better known by her religious name - Domneva. King Egbert, her uncle, gave the land to Ermenburga as compensation when her two brothers were murdered by one of his men, the thane, Thunor. Legend has it that Thunor secured the throne of Kent for Egbert by murdering the two princes, Ethelbert and Ethelred, and he buried their bodies, secretly, in the grounds of the royal palace. The graves were soon found, revealed, so it is said, by mysterious columns of light, and a penitent King Egbert let loose a deer to run free, declaring that all the land that it

encompassed by its route would be given to Ermenburga. As Thunor watched he became alarmed at the distance that the deer was covering and set out to try halt it but he fell, with his horse, into a ditch and was drowned.

In the end, Ermenburga received over 1,000 acres and the story of the manner in which it was acquired is illustrated in the windows of the parish church of St Mary. Ermenburga founded **Minster Abbey** in 670 and, although the nunnery was later sacked by the Danes, it became part of the estate of St Augustine's Abbey, Canterbury. The monks set about rebuilding the abbey, adding a grange, and much of the Norman work can still be seen in the cloisters and other parts of the ruins.

THE BELL INN

2 High Street, Minster-in-Thanet,
Kent CT12 4BU
Tel: 01843 821274

Situated just west of the Minster, on the High Street in the heart of the village, **The Bell Inn** has already enough going for it to make it worth a stop. Visitors step inside to enter a world of low oak-beam ceilings, blazing log fires, with a murmur of conversation, in this friendly village pub. First time visitors will quickly become aware of the welcoming atmosphere in this characterful establishment, which has a history dating back over 400 years, resulting in a loyal local clientele. Aleks and Ian Young have been the hosts for over seven years and know how to look after their customers. Aas well as the good selection of keg lager, cider and stout stocked behind the bar, there are also four real ales kept on tap which include well-known names as well as some local varieties. There is also a varied wine list.

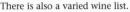

Food is available each lunch time and evening (except Sunday nights during the winter) with the menus offering a good choice of bar snacks and daily home-made specials. In the evening an a la carte menu is also available - the choices being changed approximately every two months. Both menus are at very competitive prices. The lovely garden is popular in the warmer months, with patrons lingering over their drinks while they enjoy the memorable views, or simply basking in the sunshine.

DEAL

This delightful fishing town has changed little in character since the 18th century thanks, in part, to its shingle rather than sandy beach, which meant that Deal escaped Victorian development into a full blown seaside resort. The fishing industry has always played a major role along this stretch of coastline and the roots of that trade are still very much in evidence in the town today. Deal's seafront is one of the most picturesque along the southeast coast and, with its quaint alleyways, traditional fishermen's cottages and old houses, the town is well worth exploring. Not surprisingly, given its history, Deal was also the haunt of smugglers and these illegal activities were centred around Middle Street. It was in a house along this street that, in 1801, Nelson's great friend, Captain Edward Parker, died from wounds that he received following a raid on Boulogne. Nelson was a frequent visitor to the town and, in the early 19th century, he outraged local society by staying at the Royal Hotel with his mistress, Lady Emma Hamilton.

The **Maritime and Local History Museum** is an excellent place to begin as the displays here cover many aspects of the life of the town and its people. Housed in stables that were once used to shelter army mules, the museum, in particular, has a large collection of real and model boats, figureheads, compasses and other navigational aids, pilot's relics and other memorabilia that relate to Deal's seafaring and fishing past. Meanwhile, on the site of the old Naval yard stands the distinctive **Timeball Tower** that was built in 1795 and that was used to give time signals to ships in the English Channel. The four storey building had a curious device whereby a

HOLE IN THE ROOF HOTEL AND CAFÉ BAR

42 Queen Street, Deal, Kent CT14 6EY
Tel: 01304 374839 Fax: 01304 373768

Found in the centre of the town, the **Hole in the Roof Hotel and Café Bar** is a place that is well worth taking the trouble to visit. From the outside, this seems like many other British informal restaurants but, once inside, customers will find that the curiously named Hole in the Roof has a very sophisticated and continental feel. Light and airy - because it does have a "hole in the ceiling" - the gentle colours of the walls and wooden floor help to create a peaceful and relaxing atmosphere in which customers can enjoy the excellent hospitality

on offer here. Personally run by manager Phil Bailey, this friendly and welcoming café has a well stocked bar that serves, amongst the usual drinks, real ales, stouts, ciders and wine. Food too is an

important aspects of the Hole in the Roof and the imaginative dishes put together by chef Tony Suckling are both interesting and tempting. Specialising in Italian and Mediterranean dishes, the ever changing menu also features a good range of vegetarian choices and the café's Sunday lunches, for which booking is recommended, are very popular. However, this is not all that the Hole in the Roof has to offer as, above the café bar, there are eight delightful and stylish guest rooms that are let on a bed and breakfast basis. All in all this is a charming place that knows how to look after its customers.

Deal Castle

black copper ball was dropped down its central shaft at exactly one o'clock to warn ships just off the coast to be ready to set their chronometers. Although this original system has long since been replace by a modern radio time signal, a replica ball still drops down the shaft. The tower is also home to a museum that is devoted to time and telegraphy.

Not far from the Timeball Tower stands the menacing fortress of **Deal Castle** which was built by Henry VIII in the early 1540s as one of a number of forts designed to protect the south coast from invasion by the French and Spanish, angered over Henry's divorce of his Catholic wife, Catherine of Aragon. The castle was designed to resemble a Tudor rose and the distinctive 'lily-pad' shape can only really be appreciated from the air or by looking at plans of the site. A huge bastion, Deal Castle had 119 guns trained out across the sea and it must have been a very formidable sight to anyone thinking of making an attack. Despite all these precautions, Deal Castle never came under attack from foreign invaders and it was not until the Civil War that the fortress saw action. In 1648, the castle, that was held on behalf of Charles I, came under fire from the Parliamentarians and, although it was extensively damaged, the

castle was not attacked again until it was hit by a bomb during World War II. A superb place to explore as there are long dark passages, battlement and a huge basement, the castle also has an exhibition on the castle's history and the various defensive castles that were constructed under Henry VIII. At the northern end of the town lies another of Henry VIII's great fortresses, **Sandown Castle**, but unfortunately time has not been so kind to Sandown and all that remains are some ruined buttresses.

The quiet waters just off the coast of Deal are known as **The Downs** and they create a safe anchorage for ships that might otherwise run aground on the treacherous **Goodwin Sands**. In fact, the sands, for centuries, have proved to be a graveyard for unwary vessels and the sad sight of shipwrecks, with their masts poking above the water, can still be seen at low tide. These sands were mentioned by Shakespeare, in the *Merchant of Venice*, as a place where the eponymous merchant lost one of his ships. As many as 50,000 men may have perished on these sands and there are numerous tales of 'ghost ships' that have been sighted here.

AROUND DEAL

WALMER
1½ miles S of Deal on the A258

This residential seaside town merges, almost imperceptibly with its neighbour, Deal, to the north but Walmer does have its very own, distinct, history. It is firmly believed that it was here, in 55BC, that Julius Caesar and his legions landed in England. However, the town is now best known for its sister castle to Deal,

Walmer Castle and Gardens

Younger, the Duke of Wellington and Sir Winston Churchill, and that is, today, held by HM Queen Elizabeth, The Queen Mother. A charming and delightful place, that is well liked by The Queen Mother, visitors to the castle can not only see the Duke of Wellington's rooms, and even his famous boots, but also stroll around the **Gardens**. In particular, in honour of The Queen Mother's 95th birthday (in August 1995), a special garden was planted and, along with the rest of the beautiful, well kept grounds, there is a charming tearoom. One time owners of the castle, the Beauchamp family, were the inspiration for the Flyte family that featured in Evelyn Waugh's novel *Brideshead Revisited*.

Walmer Castle that, whilst being built as one of Henry VIII's line of coastal defences in the 1540s, has become, over the years, an elegant stately home. Today it is the official residence of the Lord Warden of the Cinque Ports, a title that has been held by William Pitt the

KINGSDOWN PARK HOLIDAY VILLAGE

Kingsdown Park, Upper Street, Nr. Deal, Kent CT14 8AU
Tel: 01304 361205 Fax: 01304 380125
e-mail info@kingsdownpark.co.uk
website www.kingsdownpark.co.uk

Kingsdown Park Holiday Village enjoys a prime cliff-top location within the village of Kingsdown, between the historic towns of Deal and Dover. The holiday village is perfectly placed for exploring the delightful 'Garden of England' as well being within easy reach of the many visitor attractions and golf courses.

The complex comprises a number of A-frame Scandinavian style lodges each with a sunny veranda leading through to a large lounge/dining area with a fully equipped kitchen. The lodges vary in size sleeping from between four and six people in 2-4 bedrooms.

Within the holiday village there are a large number of facilities available to residents, mostly without charge. There is a swimming pool, with separate children's pool, tennis court, children's games room, volley ball, table tennis, crazy golf, badminton, BBQ and open play area. There is also a privately owned beach within a five minute walk which is safe for children. Guests can also enjoy use of the Clubhouse which offers a fully licensed bar and restaurants as well as hosting live entertainment, discos, quizzes and bingo. Within the site there is also a shop, for all those little essentials, and a launderette. In addition to the accommodation there are two function suites available for private parties, wedding receptions for business meetings.

RINGWOULD
3 miles S of Deal on the A258

Centuries ago, this village stood on the edge of a vast forest that extended westwards almost to the city of Canterbury. Meanwhile, the oldest building in the village is undoubtedly the 12th century **church of St Nicholas** whose curious onion dome was added to the 17th century tower to act as a navigation aid for ships out in the English Channel. The village's old forge too had maritime connections and this is where iron carriage wheels and chains were made to be used at the naval dockyard in nearby Deal.

ST MARGARET'S AT CLIFFE
5½ miles S of Deal off the A258

This small town stands on cliffs that overlook **St Margaret's Bay** and it was, before World War II, a secluded seaside resort with a number of hotels along the beach, that was also the home of playwright Noel Coward. Another famous resident, Ian Fleming, the author of the James Bond spy thrillers, later bought Coward's house. As this is the nearest point to the French coast, which lies some 21 miles away, St Margaret's has always been the traditional starting place for cross channel swimmers and, also because of its position, a gun emplacement was built here during World War II to protect the Channel and ward off any German invasion. Despite seemingly to be a relatively new settlement, St Margaret's possesses an ancient parish church, the 12th century **Church of St Margaret** of Antioch, that features interesting rounded arches and an intricately carved doorway.

Just to the south of the town lies **The Pines**, a six acre park, created in 1970, that is renowned for its trees, plants, shrubs and ornamental lake. The brainchild of a wealthy local builder and philanthropist Fred Cleary, the gardens' imaginative layout, that includes a Romany caravan, a statue of Sir Winston Churchill and a waterfall, provides the perfect setting in which to relax and enjoy the tranquil surroundings, as well as the glorious views over the White Cliffs. Opposite The Pines, and opened in 1989, is **St Margaret's Museum** that contains collections of artefacts put together by Fred Cleary and covers not only exhibits with a local or maritime theme but also many items of world-wide interest. The museum has a tea room and a gift and souvenir shop.

A little further south again lies **South Foreland Lighthouse**, the highlight of the White Cliffs and a distinctive landmark overlooking the Straits of Dover. Erected in 1843, the lighthouse was used by radio pioneer, Marconi, for his early experiments and it was from here that he made the world's first ship to shore radio transmission. A guided tour takes visitors around the lighthouse where its history can be learned and from where there are magnificent long-ranging views.

GREAT MONGEHAM
2 miles SW of Deal off the A258

Found high on the wall of the chancel of the parish church of St Martin is a helmet hanging from an iron pole that is said to have been worn at the Battle of Hastings in 1066. Meanwhile, and certainly much more credible, is a brass plaque on a pillar that bears a Greek verse that was written by the poet, Robert Bridges, in memory of his nurse who lies buried in the church.

WEST LANGDON
5 miles SW of Deal off the A256

Close to this small village can be seen the scant remains of **Langdon Abbey** that was founded in 1189 by Premonstratensian Canons. Dissolved by

Henry VIII, an inspection made here on behalf of the king in 1535 reported that the canons behaviour was immoral and that the abbot kept a mistress. That the canons were also ignorant seems to be the very least of their 'crimes'. After the dissolution, much of the masonry of the abbey was carted to the coast and used in the construction of Henry VIII's coastal defences and, later, a farmhouse was built on the abbey site.

NORTHBOURNE
3 miles W of Deal off the A256

In the church of this small country village can be found a monument to Sir Edwin Sandys who was responsible for the drawing up of the constitution of Virginia, in America, and who was born in the village at Northbourne Court. Edwin's son also made a name for himself as he became a prominent commander in the Civil War on the Parliamentarian side. Renowned for his cruelty, Colonel Edwin Sandys died in the village in 1642 as a result of the injuries he sustained during the battle of Worcester. Although the house that these two gentlemen knew was demolished in the 18th century, the **ornamental gardens** survive and they, though not the more recent residence, are occasionally open to the public.

TILMANSTONE
4½ miles W of Deal off the A256

At one time the largest mine of the East Kent coalfield, Tilmanstone Colliery, could be found just to the south of the village. When the mine closed, in 1987, this ended mining in east Kent and the site of the colliery has been turned into an industrial estate.

EASTRY
4½ miles E of Deal off the A256

Situated along the Roman road that linked Richborough with Dover, this ancient village has a couple of interesting historic connections: it was here, in 1164, that Thomas à Becket hid whilst waiting to travel to Flanders after his quarrel with Henry II; Lord Nelson also visited the village and one of his officers, Captain John Harvey, lies buried in the churchyard.

4 North Downs to Dover

Following the North Downs eastwards to the coast, this area ends, or begins, at Dover, the traditional 'Gateway to England'. As Britain's major cross Channel port, this is where many start their holiday in England (or leave to go abroad) but the town is well used to 'invaders' and, during the Roman occupation, it was at Dover that they stationed their navy. Still dominated by its castle, set high above the famous White Cliffs, this originally Norman fortress has, over the centuries, been an impressive repellent to unfriendly foes thinking of mounting an attack. Whilst the huge structure of the castle makes this is wonderful place to wander around, it is the Secret Wartime Tunnels that attract much of the attention. A labyrinthine maze of tunnels cut into the cliffs, it was here, during World War II, that evacuation of Dunkirk was masterminded by Winston Churchill and Admiral Ramsey.

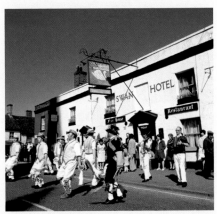

Morris Dancing

Although defence of the country from sea attack is a key aspect of this stretch of coast, it was overhead that one of the great battles of World War II took place and close to the coast are both the Battle of Britain Memorial and the Kent Battle of Britain Museum. They each play tribute, in separate ways, to the courage of the young pilots who fought unselfishly to win air supremacy over the skies of England and so prevent a German invasion.

It may seem that this area is given over to war but the idyllic nature of many of the rural villages of this region portray a picture that is both peaceful and tranquil. Very much part of the 'Garden of England', further inland lies the National Fruit Collection, where literally hundred of apples, pears, plums and numerous other fruit trees are grown, and the famous Wye College, the agricultural institution that is now part of the University of London. There are also ancient country houses that open their glorious, gardens to the public such as Beech Court Gardens and Belmont.

At the heart of the rural idyll lies Ashford that, like many places in Kent has a history that goes back to Roman times. The central location of the town has led it, over the centuries, to become a meeting place for people, farmers and travellers and, today, with the opening of the Channel Tunnel and its International Station it is beginning to rival Dover for the title 'Gateway to Britain'.

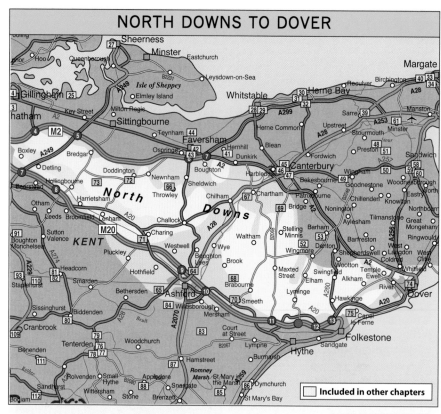

© MAPS IN MINUTES ™ (2000)

PLACES TO STAY, EAT, DRINK AND SHOP

ASHFORD

Found in the heart of the Garden of England, Ashford, which boasts some fine Georgian houses, is surrounded by countryside that has inspired such famous writers as HE Bates, Jane Austen and HG Wells. The town itself is dominated by the great central tower of its splendid 15th century parish church that rises high above the other town buildings and that has each of its four pinnacles crowned by a golden weathervane in the shape of an arrow. Ashford's central location makes it an ideal base from which to visit many of the county's attractions but it is well worth spending time here and, at the **Ashford Borough Museum**, visitors can find out more about this interesting and historic place. Housed in Dr Wilks' Hall, which was formerly the Old Grammar

Orchards around Ashford

School, the museum has a varied collection that ranges from Victorian patchwork to equipment used by the town's fire brigade.

Ashford is proud that it is the home of the first volunteer Fire Service in the country that was formed here in 1826 and which purchased its first manual fire engine some 10 years later. In 1925, the first Leyland motor fire engine went into service at Ashford and the funds required to buy the appliance were raised by public subscription. Unfortunately, the original fire station has since been demolished and replaced with shops.

The town's central location, as well as being at a major crossing point of two important routes, saw a Roman settlement established here in around the 1st century and, for several centuries before the Norman Conquest, records show that a town, called Esseteford, could be found here. Growing into a flourishing market town that served the surrounding area, Ashford developed further with the building of, first, turnpike roads and then the arrival of the railway in 1842. Today, the railway still influences the town and, with the completion of the Channel Tunnel, a range of Continental European destinations can be reached in just a few of hours from Ashford's **International Station**.

AROUND ASHFORD

BOUGHTON LEES
2½ miles N of Ashford on the A251

This delightful village, along with its neighbour Boughton Aluph, lies on the southern fringes of the North Downs, where the wooded hills give way to hedgerows, meadows, field and a network of narrow, twisting lanes. The long distance footpath, the **North Downs**

THE CROFT HOTEL

Canterbury Road, Kennington,
near Ashford, Kent TN25 4DU
Tel: 01233 622140 Fax: 01233 635271
e-mail: crofthotel@btconnect.com

Found on the outskirts of Ashford and surrounded by its own private grounds, **The Croft Hotel** is a charming establishment that prides itself on its friendly atmosphere and that is owned and personally run by Mario and Marguerite Camponeshi and their daughter Heidi.

Each of the 28 guest rooms has an en suite bathroom as well as all the usual

facilities found in larger establishments but, what The Croft Hotel also offers its guests, is intimate surroundings where guests can really feel at home. The lounge and bar are just the places to enjoy a quiet drink and conversation with other guests before moving through to the dining room. The theme in the dining room is Italian and as Mario, the chef, comes from Rome, guests can be sure that all the Italian dishes served here are authentic. Meanwhile, the menu also features dishes from around the world and there is a special children's menu. Finally, The Croft Hotel is an excellent place for a wedding reception, when the garden really comes into its own, and, along with family, manger Christopher Cox is on hand to ensure guests have a pleasant and enjoyable stay.

THE SWAN

The Street, Great Chart, near Ashford, Kent TN23 3AN
Tel: 01233 623250

The Swan is a typical Kentish style building has a striking Dutch gable that ensures that anyone passing through Great Chart is such to notice this popular inn. As well as the lawned area to the front, there is a small beer garden to the rear of the inn where too can be found ample car parking. Meanwhile, inside The Swan is a traditional and unspoilt inn that provides a comfortable environment in which to enjoy the hospitality of landlord Christopher Baker.

Low ceilings add to the intimacy around the open plan bar area and the comfortable leather

armchairs and shelves of books suggest that is just the place to settle down with a pint and have a good read. As well as the excellent range of beers, lagers and real ales here there is an extensive menu of traditional English pub food available. From sandwiches through to home-made beef and stilton pie - a particular favourite here - there is sure to be plenty to tickle the tastebuds. Served throughout the week at both lunchtimes and in the evenings (except Sunday and Monday), Sunday lunchtime sees the addition of traditional roasts.

A popular place with both locals and visitors, the monthly live music evenings also draw people here.

Way, makes the descent from the higher ground at this point and it passes right alongside the parish church of Boughton Aluph. A similar network of footpaths and narrow lanes leads southwards to Boughton Lees.

CHALLOCK
4½ miles N of Ashford off the A251

This pretty village, centred around its wide and spacious green, is set in the dense woodlands known as **Challock Forest**. Like so many villages with its roots in the Middle Ages, Challock was built around its church in a forest clearing. However, when the Black Plague struck, the villagers moved to a new site, a mile or so from the church. Dedicated to Saints Cosmus and Damian, the church was the victim of a direct bomb hit during World War II and, now restored, it is worth visiting, not just for its location but also because some fine wall paintings were added in the 1950s as part of the restoration.

Set around a medieval farmhouse, **Beech Court Gardens** provides something of interest for everyone right throughout the seasons. A riot of colour in the spring when the azaleas, vibernums and rhododendrons are in flower, the garden has brilliant summer borders and roses whilst, in the autumn, there are the rich tones of the acers. Well known for its relaxing atmosphere, the garden has more than 90 named trees, woody areas and extensive lawns.

Meanwhile, just to the south of the village lies **Eastwell Park** with its 40 acre lake that provides a counterpoint for the manor house that is in private hands. On the northern edge of the lake is a ruined church that reputedly houses the bones of Richard Plantagenet, son of Richard III. According to local legend, in the mid 15th century, when Sir Thomas Moyle was building his new mansion on the estate, he was surprised to find that his foreman bricklayer was reading a book in Latin. Thomas asked the bricklayer where he received his education and was told that in 1485, when he was a young man, the bricklayer had been summoned to Bosworth Field where he was told that he had received such an education as he was the illegitimate son of Richard III and the king was ready to acknowledge him as his rightful heir. The next day, at the Battle of Bosworth, Richard III was killed and the

Eastwell Park

king's son fled the battlefield. Disguising himself as a humble bricklayer to avoid being recognised by Tudor men, the king's son continued at this trade from then onwards. Moved by the story, Thomas gave the man a house on the estate and, after his death, had this entry made in the burial register: "December 22, 1550: Richard Plantagenet."

THROWLEY
7½ miles N of Ashford off the A251

Tucked away amid the orchards of Kent and close to the village lies **Belmont** a beautiful Georgian mansion house and estate. The work of the architect, Samuel Wyatt, the house has managed to remain completely unspoilt and, since 1801, it has been the home of successive Lords Harris. Renowned for its impressive clock collection, the house is home to numerous artefacts that the family have collected from overseas along with some fine furniture and paintings. The surrounding grounds contain an equally impressive walled garden, a pinetum and an Orangery (see panel below).

SHELDWICH
8½ miles N of Ashford on the A251

Standing at the point where the landscape blends gently from scattered woodlands to open meadows and then farms and orchards, Sheldwich has, at its centre, a Norman parish church with a distinctive squat steeple that is visible from miles around. Meanwhile, just to the north, at **Brogdale**, can be found the **National Fruit Collection** that moved here some 30 years ago. Home to the largest collection of fruit trees and plants in the world, visitors here can see over 2,300 varieties of apples, 550 pears, and numerous plums, cherries and bush fruits along with smaller collections of nuts and vines that are all grown in the beautiful orchards. Particularly spectacular when the blossom is out, there are guided tours around the fruit collections and visitors are given the chance to see new varieties such as apples that taste like pineapples, crab apples that can be pickled and 'Beurre' pears that have been cultivated in Belgium to melt in the mouth! The

BELMONT

Belmont Park, Throwley, Faversham, Kent ME13 0HH
Tel: 01795 890202

Commanding stunning views across the rolling Kent countryside, **Belmont** is a marvellous example of Georgian architecture that has remained completely unspoilt. Until Edward Wilks, the store-keeper of the Royal Powder Mills at Faversham bought this land in 1769 there was no house or estate of Belmont. The house that he had built still survives as a wing of the present building and that in turn was constructed to the designs of Samuel Wyatt between 1789 and 1793 for the new owner, Colonel John Montresor of the Royal Engineers. It was the Colonel who is responsible for creating much of the estate seen today but, unfortunately, his career ended prematurely when he was accused of embezzlement and, in 1801, the estate was purchased, at auction, by General George Harris, with money earned during his successful military career in India.

Created a lord in 1815 following his victory at Seringapatam, he and successive Lords Harris have continued to live at Belmont and also play a distinguished role in the expansion of the British Empire. As soldier and colonial governors stationed around the world, the family has acquired a vast range of mementoes from overseas that can be seen on display throughout the house. Whilst the artefacts are certainly decorative and interesting it would be a mistake not to also take in the delightfully well proportioned rooms of this lovely Georgian mansion along with the paintings and fine furniture. However, it is the magnificent clock collection put together by the 5th Lord Harris that takes pride of place and it is the most extensive to be found in private hands.

Meanwhile, the surrounding gardens are equally impressive and here there is not only a walled garden and a pinetum, with a Victorian Shell Grotto, but also an Orangery, designed as an extension to the house, that is planted with orange trees, palms and other tropical trees.

Brogdale Plant Centre, which is open throughout the year, sells many varieties of fruit for visitors to take home.

BOUGHTON
10½ miles N of Ashford off the A2

Although close to the main road and other major routes to Kent's coast, it is well worth pausing a while here and exploring **Farming World at Nash Court**. Almost every aspect of farming is mentioned here, one way or another, and, with beautiful surrounding countryside and marked trails for walking, there is plenty here to keep the whole family amused for hours. Farming World's extensive breeding programme ensures that there are usually lots of young animals here, such as lambs, kids, calves and chicks, but it is also home to a variety of rarer breeds like miniature Shetland ponies, llamas and Britain's smallest breed of cattle.

Along with the animals, the birds of prey and the heavy horses, Farming World is home to a **Museum** where a fascinating collection of agricultural implements are on display. Throughout the year there are demonstrations on the ancient and traditional skills of farming and other crafts whilst specialist talks on a range of subjects, including bee keeping, animal husbandry and falconry, are also held here.

CHILHAM
7½ miles NE of Ashford on the A252

This well preserved village is one of Kent's show piece places and, particularly the area around the village square, is often used as a location for filming. The houses here are primarily Tudor and Jacobean and they are a delightfully haphazard mix of gabled, half-timbered houses, shops and ancient inns that date from the Middle Ages. A stopping place for

STOUR FARM

Riverside, Chartham, Canterbury, Kent CT4 7NX
Tel: 01227 731977 Fax: 01227 731977
e-mail: info@stourfarm.co.uk
website: stourfarm.co.uk

Found on the outskirts of the village, and just a couple of miles from Canterbury, **Stour Farm** is the ideal place for a relaxing break in the heart of some of Kent's most beautiful and historic countryside. An attractive barn conversion, the house overlooks the River Stour and, from here, owners Jane and Jeremy Wilson offer superb bed and breakfast accommodation in a choice of two comfortable en suite guest rooms. A further studio style twin room is also available and this is let on a self-catering basis. The rooms are, like the rest of the house, tastefully decorated and furnished and all the facilities today's traveller would expect are provided. A full home-cooked breakfast is served in the separate guests'

dining room or, if the weather permits, out on the sun terrace that looks out over the riverbank. Despite being secluded and tranquil, Stour Farm is conveniently situated for many of the area's places of interest and the local pub, which serves dinner, is only a short walk away. Stour Farm welcomes children over 12 years of age.

BULLTOWN FARMHOUSE

Bulltown Lane, West Brabourne,
Kent TN25 5NB
Tel: 01233 813505
Fax: 01277 709544

Formerly part of the estate of Lord Brabourne, **Bulltown Farmhouse** is a lovely old house that dates back to the 15th century. Found in a secluded setting, this charming place is the home of Lilly and Julian Wilton who have also restored the wonderful building to create a splendid family home. Since 1997, this friendly and personable couple have been offering excellent bed and breakfast accommodation for guests in three superb en suite rooms. Each of the rooms have glorious views from the windows, either over the north Downs or the house's walled garden, and all are decorated and furnished to the same high standard as the rest of the house.

Downstairs, there is a visitors' lounge where the beamed ceiling and the wood burning stove in the large inglenook fireplace all add to the traditional country atmosphere of Bulltown Farmhouse. The heavily beamed dining room is similar and, whilst being served a home-cooked breakfast, guests can again enjoy the views. Ideal for anyone seeking a secluded place to stay, Bulltown Farmhouse also appeals to those walking the north Downs and Pilgrims Way - both of which are nearby. This too is an excellent place for children as Lilly and Julian have two young daughters and there is a large cottage garden surrounding the house.

THE GRANVILLE

Street End Road, Lower Hardres, Canterbury, Kent CT4 7AL
Tel: 01227 700402 Fax: 01227 700261 website: www.shepherd-neame.co.uk

Found on the main road through the village, **The Granville** is an attractive old inn that is, today, one of Shepherd Neame Brewery's premier houses. Managed by Andrew and Shirley Allen, a very hospitable couple with over 25 years experience in the licensing trade, this delightful inn has plenty to offer its customers. Recently refurbished, the interior of The Granville is a gentle mix of ancient and modern where the light, bright colours give the inn an airy feel whilst the old furniture and some of the building's original features add a sense of continuity. As well as offering a full range of real ales, including Shepherd Neame's Masterbrew and Spitfire, there is a superb menu served here.

The delicious mix of dishes is created by chef Stephen Hann and the style is very much traditional English given a new and exciting twist. The menu is served throughout the week but it is essential to book at weekends and on special occasions as The Granville is becoming increasingly popular as its reputation spreads.

Chilham in the Snow

pilgrims on their way to the shrine of Thomas à Becket in Canterbury Cathedral, Chilham today plays host to other visitors who, now, walk the nearby **North Downs Way**.

The village is also the home of **Chilham Castle** that originally consisted of a Norman keep built on Roman foundations although a Jacobean mansion house was added by Sir Dudley Digges, an official of James I. The spacious grounds around the castle were first laid out by Charles I's gardener, John Tradescan, but they were reworked in the 18th century by Capability Brown. Meanwhile, the lodge gates, that can be found in the village square, were added in the 20th century. It was close to Chilham that the Romans fought their last great battle in Britain and the site is known as Julieberrie Downs in honour of Julius Laberius who was killed there in 54BC.

BRIDGE
12½ miles NE of Ashford off the A2

The village stands at a river crossing, where the old Dover Road from London crosses a tributary of the River Stour, and this is, obviously, the source of the village's name. Now by-passed by the main A2 dual carriageway, this village was, for many years, subjected to a

constant stream of heavy traffic and the villagers, in the 1970s, caused such a bottleneck whilst protesting to have the road through the village re-routed that the government relented and the by-pass was opened in 1976.

Close to the bridge lies a mansion that was altered for Count Zabrowski of *Chitty Chitty Bang Bang* fame.

STELLING MINNIS
8 miles NE of Ashford off the B2068

Found on the edge of what remains of the once great Lyminge Forest, this village has an attractive rural atmosphere. Minnis means 'common' and today's open spaces here reflect a sense of preservation that the Victorians applied not only to the village itself but also to its church as this was not overly restored in the 19th century. On the outskirts of Stelling Minnis stands **Davison's Mill**, a smock mill built in 1866 that continued to grind corn commercially until 1970. The mill wheels were rotated by either wind or the mill's 1912 Ruston and Hornsby oil engine and the museum here has displays of some of the original mill maintenance tools along with other milling implements.

WYE
3 miles NE of Ashford off the A28

This attractive old market town, on the North Downs, has some fine Georgian houses as well as some half-timbered buildings in the area surrounding its 15th century collegiate church. However, it is not these buildings that have made the town famous but its agricultural college - **Wye College**, that is now affiliated to the University of London. Occupying the buildings of a priests' college that was built in 1447 by John Kempe, Archbishop of Canterbury, the college, in early 2001, fell foul of animal rights' protesters who stole their hunt's pack of hounds.

THE WOOLPACK

Church Road, Smeeth,
near Ashford, Kent TN25 6RX
Tel: 01303 812196
Fax: 01303 812942

The Woolpack is a welcoming local pub in the village of Smeeth near Ashford. Tenants Rod and Judy Vidler have run The Woolpack since May 1997 but they have lived in Smeeth for more than 20 years and they are a popular pair. This is the sort of pub that forms the heart of a small community, and on a given evening - or lunchtime - new customers might find themselves rubbing shoulders with darts players, members of the quiz team, or the village cricketers slaking their thirst. There is even a chance to try bat and trap, a local Kentish game.

Oak panelling throughout gives a warm feeling to the interior, helped by a double-sided open fire. Outside is a large garden with many attractions for children and a special barbecue patio for summer meals. A selection of hearty pub food is matched by a choice of real and cask ales. Always looking to provide more for their customers, Rod and Judy now have a take away service, for both fish and chips and pizza, which is available from Monday to Saturday lunchtimes and most evenings. Orders can either be telephoned through to the inn or, and perhaps more popularly, taken at the bar where a quick drink can be enjoyed whilst the food is being prepared.

THE PILGRIMS TABLE

19 High Street, Charing Village,
Kent TN27 0HU
Tel: 01233 712170
Fax: 01233 712170

Although **The Pilgrims Table**, on Charing's main street, only opened in April 2000, it has already made a mark: by winning the Taste of Kent competition. Presenting a menu that combined many different flavours that illustrated the wealth of local ingredients, this charming and relaxed bistro-style restaurant has certainly gone from strength to strength and anyone dining here will be treated to a very special meal indeed.

Owned by Sigrid Van Dijk, this historic 15th century building, which lies on an old pilgrims' route, has a traditional, almost medieval, theme, with exposed beams, open fires and tapestries hanging from the walls. During the day, The Pilgrims Table is a popular and delightful tea rooms where, as well as serving a full range of tasty and tempting snacks and light meals, there is a long list of teas and coffees from which to choose. In the evening the mood changes as does the menu, as the candles are lit, and diners are treated to a wide ranging menu in a modern British style although the influences of both continental and oriental cuisine can be seen. Whatever the time of day, The Pilgrims Table is a superb place to come to for an enjoyable and interesting meal. The Pilgrims Table is open from Wednesday to Sunday.

BROOK
3 miles E of Ashford off the A28

A scattered village in the wooded farmland that lies beneath the North Downs, Brook is home to an **Agricultural Museum** that occupies old farm buildings that stand on a site that dates back to Saxon times. Originally beginning as a small collection of farm implements and tools that were in the hands of nearby Wye College, the collection has grown and it now includes such items as ploughs, man traps, shepherd's crooks and domestic artefacts like butter pats and flat irons. However, it is not just the collection that is of interest here as two of the buildings in which the displays can be seen are worthy of special note. The barn was constructed in the 1370s and its oak framework is particularly interesting as, not only is it original, but it also reveals the skills of the craftsmen involved in its construction. Meanwhile, the oast house, that dates from 1815, is an early example of one with a round kiln - that were thought to give the hops more even drying - and it is possibly unique in having four fireplaces rather that just a single one.

SMEETH
4½ miles SE of Ashford on the A20

A charming and traditional Kentish village, where traditional games are still played, Smeeth's name means 'a smooth clearing in the woods' and though, today, most of the woods have long since gone remains of ancient forests, such as Lyminge to the north, can still be found.

WILLESBOROUGH
1½ miles SE of Ashford off the A20

Now almost swallowed up by the expansion of Ashford, this once rural village is home to **Willesborough Windmill**, a smock mill that dates back to 1869 and which was restored in 1991.

Visitors here can take a guided tour around the mill and see just what life was like for a miller at the beginning of the 20th century whilst the mill is also home to a collection of artefacts that relate to Ashford's industrial heritage.

WESTWELL
2½ miles NW of Ashford off the A20

Now a quiet village, Westwell was originally a Saxon settlement that was further developed by the Normans who built the lovely parish church.

CHARING
5 miles NW of Ashford on the A20

There has been a settlement here for centuries as there are a line of springs close to the village and the earliest evidence is that of an Iron Age flint workings. Archaeologists suggest that there could well have been a Roman villa close by and the village's name is said to be derived from that of a local Jutish chief. In the late 8th century, Charing was given to Canterbury Cathedral by Egbert II, King of Kent, and the manor here remained the property of the archbishops until 1545 when Henry VIII confiscated it from Archbishop Cramner.

Charing Countryside

The little that remains of this archbishop's palace today dates from the early 14th century and many of the buildings have been incorporated into a private farm. However, when visiting the parish church of St Peter and St Paul in the village, the archbishop still robes in this ancient palace.

The village, which lies one day's journey from Canterbury and Charing, became one of the many stopping places, in the Middle Ages, where pilgrims would seek rest, shelter and food whilst on their pilgrimage. This was also the home of a flourishing market, that stood in the traditional place, just outside the gates of the manor house, and, due to its antiquity, it never required a charter.

Oast Houses, Lenham

PLUCKLEY
5½ miles NW of Ashford off the A20

This little village clusters around a tidy little square and the surrounding cottages all have a curious feature - 'Dering' windows. These were added by a 19th century landowner who thought the style particularly lucky as one of his ancestors had escaped through such a window

THE OLD SCHOOL HOUSE

Church Hill, Doddington, near Sittingbourne, Kent ME9 0BD
Tel: 01795 890484

Found adjacent to St John's Church and just a few minutes walk from Doddington village, **The Old School House** is a beautifully converted building that was originally used as the Sunday school. A quiet and peaceful location, this charming cottage provides comfortable holiday accommodation on two floors and, throughout, The Old School House has been furnished and decorated to a very high standard in a pleasing country style. A double bedroom and bathroom lie on the ground floor

whilst the fully fitted modern kitchen and the lounge (with a sofa bed) are upstairs.

From this elevated position there are glorious views over the secluded and private garden and beyond to Doddington Place Gardens that lie next door to the cottage. A utility room and further single bedroom can be found adjacent to the cottage. The ideal place for a family - children over five are welcome - the large and well tendered garden is perfect place for enjoy a pre dinner drink on a summer's evening whilst the cottage is a delightful home from home.

Doddington Gardens

during the Civil War. He also put them into his own mansion but this appears to be where his luck ended as the great house burnt down.

DODDINGTON
10 miles NW of Ashford off the A2

The landscaped gardens of **Doddington Place**, in this traditional little rural village, are truly magnificent and comprise

RINGLESTONE INN FARMHOUSE HOTEL

Ringlestone Hamlet, near Harrietsham,
Maidstone, Kent ME17 1NX
Tel: 01622 859900 Fax: 01622 859966
e-mail: bookings@ringlestone.com
website: www.ringlestone.com

Found deep in the heart of the North Downs and yet close to many of the attractions of the local area, including Leeds Castle just a few minutes drive away, **Ringlestone Inn Farmhouse Hotel** is an idyllic place that is very much off the beaten track. Dating back to 1533, the inn was originally built by monks as a hospice and it became one of the early ale houses in around 1615. Little has changed here since those days and the inn retains many of its original features such as the brick and flint walls and floors, aged oak beams, inglenook fireplaces and old English furniture. Even the addition of a dining room has not changed the atmosphere and style of the place and the table here were specially made from the timbers of an 18th century Thames barge. Guests at the inn can see, on the English oak sideboard, the inscription, "A Ryghte Joyouse and welcome greetynge to ye all", and this is as true today as it was in 1632 when the words were carved.

Along with the more usual drinks served here, Ringlestone is noted for its wide range of English country fruit wines

and liqueurs. There is also an excellent wine list that complements the superb cuisine. The daily hot and cold buffet lunches offer a vast selection of dishes that make the very best of seasonal foods whilst, in the intimate surroundings of the candlelit dining room, guests can enjoy an equally exceptional dinner from the extensive á la carte menu that feature the inn's famous pies. Finally, the inn's three guest bedrooms provide the perfect setting for a comfortable and relaxing night's sleep.

lawns, avenues and clipped yew hedges. The display of rhododendrons and azaleas in the spring is brilliant whilst there are also large rock gardens and a formal sunken garden to view. There is a gift shop here along with a restaurant.

HARRIETSHAM
11 miles NW of Ashford on the A20

A pleasant village with views stretching southwards over the Weald of Kent and with the North Downs as a backdrop. However, before the completion of the M20 motorway, life in the village was much less peaceful as the A20, that cuts it into two, was the major route between Maidstone and Folkestone and the other Channel ports.

HOLLINGBOURNE
13 miles NW of Ashford off the A20

Along with the adjoining hamlet, **Eythorne Street**, Hollingbourne forms a linear village stretching out below the rising North Downs. Of the two, Eythorne Street is the older and here a number of timber-framed and traditional, weatherboarded houses can be found.

DETLING
16 miles NW of Ashford off the A249

Sheltered by the North Downs and by-passed by the main road, this village has remained relatively unspoilt and, today, it is visited by many walking the nearby **Pilgrims Way** footpath. In earlier times, this was an important coaching stop on several major routes that linked Maidstone with Sittingbourne, Faversham and other towns to the north. The High Street, that had been the main thoroughfare for the stagecoaches, is now more tranquil and along here, and elsewhere in the village, there are quaint old cottages to be found. On top of nearby Delting Hill lies the **Kent County Agricultural Show Ground**, the venue

for the county's major annual agricultural, and social, event, and where also some World War II buildings still remain from the days when this site was used as an airfield.

BOXLEY
18 miles NW of Ashford off the A249

Very much a hidden village, as it lies tucked away below the North Downs and surrounded by major roads and motorways, Boxley is a small and traditional village of weatherboarded and red brick cottages. Just outside the village, to the west, lie the remains of **Boxley Abbey** that is now part of a private house and not open to the public although the abbey's late 13th century ragstone barn can be seen from the road.

Back in the village stands the 13th century **All Saints' Church**, that still retains some features from the original Norman building, and inside visitors can see a monument that recalls the gratitude of one of the village's residents had for a cat! In 1483, Sir Henry Wyatt was imprisoned in the Tower of London for denying Richard III's claim to the throne of England. Sir Henry was left to starve to death in one of the tower's cold, damp cells but a cat, by sleeping on his chest at night and bringing him pigeons to eat during the day, saved his life.

DOVER

This ancient town, which is often referred to as the 'Gateway to England', is Britain's major cross Channel port and, as well as the freight traffic, it is from Dover that many holidaymakers set out for France and beyond whilst others arrive looking to explore England. As a result, few stay in and around Dover and, with a long history that goes back to Roman times, it is well worth making the effort to do so.

Dover Harbour

It was the Romans who first developed Dover, basing their navy here, and from then on, right up to the present day, the town has relied on shipping and seafaring for its prosperity. A founder member of the Confederation of Cinque Ports that was founded by Edward I, as the old harbour silted up so the new harbour was constructed, out into the English Channel, in the 19th century. Much of the older parts of Dover were destroyed by enemy bombs during both World Wars but, in amongst the jumble of modern streets, some of the surviving ancient buildings can still be found.

Situated high on a hill above the cliff tops, and dominating the town from almost every angle, stands **Dover Castle** that dates back to 1180. Although the castle was begun by William the Conqueror it was under Henry II that the great keep was constructed and the fortress was completed by another surrounding wall which was studded with square towers and two barbicans. Throughout its long life the castle has had an interesting history and one event, in particular, occurred towards the end of the reign of King John. By 1216, the barons had become increasingly frustrated with their

king and they invited the heir to the French throne, Prince Louis, to invade and take over. He landed with his army at Dover and laid siege to the castle that was, at that time, held by Hubert de Burgh, a baron loyal to King John. Powerful though the castle's walls were, however, the French managed to gain access to the outer barbican and began to undermine the gate to the inner enclosure. At this point, King John died and the barons declared their allegiance to his successor, Henry III, and Louis went home empty handed.

Today, the castle has much to offer the visitor and, as well as it being the home of the **Princess of Wales' Royal Regiment Museum**, there are also the remains of a Roman lighthouse and a small Saxon church within the grounds. However, one of the most spectacular sights here and, one of World War II's best kept secrets, are the **Secret Wartime Tunnels** that were cut into Dover's famous white cliffs. Now open to the public and reconstructed to provide the most realistic wartime experience possible, it was in this labyrinth of tunnels that Winston Churchill and Admiral Ramsey masterminded the evacuation of nearly 350,000 troops from the beaches of

Dover Castle

Dover Castle

Dunkirk. Also in this maze of caves was an operating theatre and underground hospital and, as the lights dim and bombs drop overhead, the atmosphere of wartime Britain is brought back to life.

Back in the heart of Dover, in New Street, can be found another of Dover's popular attractions - the **Roman Painted House**. An exceptionally well preserved town house, that is thought to date from around AD 200, the building was used as a hotel for official travellers and the excavated remains have revealed extensive wall paintings and an elaborate under-floor heating system. Only discovered in 1970, the house, which has a Roman fort wall built through it, is covered by a modern structure that also houses a major display on Roman Dover (see panel below).

At first sight, the Victorian Town Hall may not seem to require special attention but this rather indifferent building incorporates the magnificent **Maison Dieu**, a hostel for Canterbury pilgrims that was founded in the early 13th century. Meanwhile, beneath the building lies the gruesome **Dover Old Town Gaol** where the horrors of Victorian prison life can be experienced. Now fully restored, the tour of the old gaol begins in the Court Room, where Thomas Wells can be seen being convicted of shooting dead a stationmaster, a crime for which he was later hanged. Visitors then have the chance to meet other inmates (using the latest 'talking head' technology), such as the young rabbit thieves and the cunning trickster, before trying out a cell that measures just six feet by four feet for themselves! Once again 'on the outside', visitors can find numerous souvenirs, gifts and items of Victoriana at the Gaol Shop.

In the Market Square can be found the area's largest and newest museum, **Dover Museum** that has an amazing range of items that illustrate the history of the town from prehistoric times onwards. There are artefacts from the time that Dover was a Roman port and fortress,

DOVER ROMAN PAINTED HOUSE

New Street, Dover, Kent
Tel: 01304 203279

The Roman Painted House, often dubbed Britain's buried Pompeii, dates from AD 200 and, although it was demolished in 270 by the army to make way for a fortress, it has been remarkably well preserved. Now covered by a modern building, this excavated site reveals is excellent detail the layout of the house as well as its underfloor heating system. Originally the walls of the house were decorated with wall paintings and these have, miraculously, survived whilst the displays surrounding the excavation site not only explain the discovery of this painted house but also the development of Roman Dover.

White Cliffs, Dover

along with finds from one of the most important archaeological sites in Britain, the nearby Buckland Saxon cemetery. The story of Dover as a Cinque Port, the town through both World Wars and numerous Victorian objects all add to the interesting picture of the town that the museum portrays. However, one of the newest displays is one of the museum's oldest as, after seven years conservation, a Bronze Age Boat, that is 3,500 years old, can also be seen here. Opposite the museum is the **White Cliffs Experience** where visitors can step back in to time of the Roman invasion and also relive the dark days of Dover during World War II. Overlooking the Straits of Dover and one of world's busiest shipping lanes, this internationally famous attraction is an excellent way to get to know the 'Gateway to Britain'.

Meanwhile, just away from the town centre, lies **The Western Heights**, a vast area that stands on what was one of the largest and strongest fortresses in the country. Dating from the late 18th and early 19th centuries, and a time when England was expecting to have to defend its shores from French invasion forces, the huge complex has been preserved to include, along with many of the defensive structures, much of the wildlife and the plants that have since colonised the site. The first buildings were erected here in the summer of 1779 and, when Napoleon posed a threat from France, further work was undertaken, in 1804, to strengthen and fortify the area further. There is the Drop Redoubt, a sunken fortress of the early 19th century that could fire guns in all directions; the 19th century three gun emplacement; St Martin's Battery, that was upgraded and saw service during World War II; and the 12th century Wayside Chapel that is thought to have been erected by Dover Priory - to name but a few of the buildings of interest here.

One final place of interest, particularly to those who remember World War II, is the **Women's Land Army Museum**, housed on a farm, that pays tribute to those ladies who served their country by working on the land. Among the numerous exhibits on display are personal letters, uniforms and a wealth of factual information.

AROUND DOVER

CAPEL LE FERNE
5 miles SW of Dover off the B2011

This village, that lies close to the cliffs between Folkestone and Dover, is home to the **Battle of Britain Memorial** that commemorates the 1940 air battle that took place in the skies overhead. The memorial includes a stone figure of a pilot in a contemplative attitude and it pays tribute to the bravery and sacrifice of the young men who unselfishly served their country. There is a visitors' centre, a Hunting Lodge, where a range of attractive souvenirs can be purchased (see panel below).

HAWKINGE
6 miles SW of Dover on the A260

Close to the village, at Hawkinge Airfield, can be found the **Kent Battle of Britain Museum** that is the home of the country's largest collection of 1940 related artefacts on display to the public. Along with the full size replicas of the planes that played such a part in the battle - a Hurricane, Spitfire and Messerschmitt have been painstakingly rebuilt from as many original parts as possible - the museum

houses an important collection of both British and German flying equipment of that era. Many of the items on display have been recovered from aircraft whichwere shot down, on both sides, and there are also weapons, vehicles and exhibits relating to the home front to see here.

ALKHAM
4 miles W of Dover off the A20

Fortunately, plans to turn this charming village, in the steep Alkham Valley, into a large residential area for miners working in the expanding East Kent coalfield never came to fruition and the village remains much as it has done for centuries. A good place from which to begin a walk in the pleasant countryside around this coastal chalk downland, Alkham is also a pleasant place to stroll around as it has retained its Norman church, 18th century Rectory,

THE BATTLE OF BRITAIN MEMORIAL

Capel le Ferne, Folkestone, Kent

On a spectacular clifftop position can be found the Battle of Britain Memorial that was built to commemorate those who fought and lost their lives in the summer of 1940. Taking the form of an immense three bladed propeller cut into the chalk hillside with, at its centre, the statue of a lone seated airman, this is a fitting tribute to those young men who so bravely and unselfishly served their country. The memorial was unveiled by HM Queen Elizabeth the Queen Mother in 1993 and an annual memorial day is held here on the Sunday that lies closest to 10th July, the start of the air battle.

The siting of the memorial here is particularly poignant as it was in the skies above, in the summer of 1940, that the RAF struggled to gain air supremacy over the Luftwaffe and so prevent the otherwise inevitable German invasion. The battle, that cost so many their lives, lasted until the end of October and, as well as being the last major conflict over British soil, the victory marked the turning point of World War II. Close to the memorial, by the flagpole that originally stood at RAF Biggin Hill, is a memorial wall on which Winston Churchill's immortal words, "Never in the field of human conflict was so much owed by so many to so Few", are carved. At the adjacent visitors' centre visitors can purchase a range of souvenirs and it should be remembered that this memorial and the site on which it stands relies on public donation for its maintenance.

ancient houses and, perhaps most importantly, its old coaching inn.

SWINGFIELD
6½ miles W of Dover on the A260

At **MacFarlanes Butterfly and Garden Centre** visitors can walk around the tropical green houses which not only contain exotic plants but also many varieties of colourful butterflies from all over the world that are allowed to fly freely. Whatever the season, there is something to see here and the life cycle of the butterfly, from the courtship displays, through the egg and caterpillar stages, to the chrysalis and finally the butterfly, are explained and can be observed at close quarters. Meanwhile, the exotic plants on which the butterflies live - such as bougainvillaea, banana and oleander - can also be studied whilst there is a garden centre, gift shop and tea rooms on the site.

ELHAM
9 miles W of Dover off the A260

This relatively unspoilt village, whose name is pronounced 'Eelham', is the starting point for a number of footpaths that lead through the Elham Valley. The disused railway line which runs through the village, during World War II, carried an 18-inch 'Boche Buster' gun (that was actually of World War I vintage) that fired shells which were seven feet long.

Found in the heart of the Elham Valley, a designated Area of Outstanding Natural Beauty, lies Parsonage Farm and its **Rural Heritage Centre**. The farm here has a long history that dates back to medieval times and it also has connections with the University of Oxford. The heritage centre explores over 600 years of history that are associated with the farm and many of the traditional farm animals seen here are old and rare breeds. After, watching the

sheep, cattle, pigs, horses and other animals, there is the peace and quiet of the old **Elham Valley railway trail** that provides the opportunity to observe the amazing number of wild mammals, birds, insects and plant life that have made their home along this long since disused track. With plenty to keep young children amused, a small rural museum, Grandfather George Palmer's old office in the medieval undercroft, the photographs and implements that explain past and present cereal production on the farm and the barns of old farming equipment, there is certainly something for everyone at **Parsonage Farm**.

RIVER
1 mile NW of Dover on the A2

Now more a suburb of Dover, this village stands on the banks of a river that has, over the centuries, powered several mills as its meanders its way out to sea. Of those long ago mills **Crabble Corn Mill** survives and this beautiful Georgian mill (dating from 1812) is still set to work on a regular basis. Visitors here can not only join the guided tour of the windmill and see the unique set of automatic 19th century flour mill machinery but also enjoy home-made meals from the mill's café. Just to the southwest of the village lie the ruins of the 12th century **St Radigunds Abbey** that was founded by French monks.

WHITFIELD
2 miles NW of Dover on the A2

For centuries this village has stood at an important crossroads where the routes to Canterbury, Dover and Sandwich met and it was also home to several manor houses. One of the ancient Lords of the Manor, Archer's Court, had one particularly unusual service in that it was his duty to hold the king's head whenever he made a

Channel crossing and support him through any seasickness to which he might succumb. This village, which is now more a suburb of Dover, is home to the **Dover Transport Museum** where a whole range of vehicles, from bicycles to buses, can be seen along with model railways and tramways. Offering a history of the local transport, the museum also includes exhibits on the East Kent coalfield and the area's maritime heritage.

TEMPLE EWELL
2½ miles NW of Dover off the A2

This ancient village, in the valley of the River Dour, was mentioned in a charter as long ago as 772 and for centuries it came under the control of successive religious orders: first the Knights Templar and then the Knights of the Order of St John of Jerusalem. As with the village of River, further down the River Dour, there were two mills in the valley here that were driven by the Dour's waters.

WOOTTON
6½ miles NW of Dover off the A260

This village was the home of Thomas Digges, the inventor of the early telescope, who, during the reign of Elizabeth I, was the builder of the original harbour complex at Dover which is now incorporated into the Western Docks. Unfortunately, nothing remains of the manor house here that was Digges home and that was demolished in 1952.

DENTON
7 miles NW of Dover on the A260

In this charming village, with a green surrounded by pretty half-timbered cottages, can be found **Denton Court** where the poet, Thomas Grey, was a frequent visitor. Close by are two other interesting, historic houses and **Broome Park**, that dates from 1635, was, at one time, the home of Field Marshall Lord Kitchener, the World War I military leader who drowned at sea after a U-boat attack in 1915. The other house, **Tappington Hall**, is said to be the oldest inhabited building in Kent and, so legend has it, it was here that the knights who killed Thomas à Becket hid after their murderous deed. Not surprisingly, the hall is associated with several ghost stories and one suggests that it is haunted by a Royalist who was killed during the Civil War by his brother who was fighting for the Parliamentarian cause.

BARHAM
8½ miles NW of Dover off the As

The village is set in a delightful river valley near the point where the woodlands of the North Downs give way to the flatter agricultural lands. This area was mentioned in the Arthurian legends as being the site of a great battle and the land around the village was used as a military camp in the early 19th century when an invasion by Napoleon was anticipated.

5 Woodlands and Marshes

This southernmost area of Kent is characterised by two diverse landscapes: the woodland, or once wooded, area around Tenterden and the marshlands of Romney and Welland. Often dubbed the 'Jewel in the Weald', Tenterden lies on the eastern border of the Weald and this place, like other villages and towns close by, has the suffix '-den' that indicates a former setting in a woodland clearing. Developed on the wealth of the woollen trade in the Middle Ages and then becoming a key market place for the area, Tenterden has a pleasing mix of old buildings and it is an excellent place to begin a tour of southern Kent. Around it are numerous charming villages and one in particular that stands out is Biddenden. However, attractive though this village undoubtedly is, it is for the Biddenden Maids, 12th century Siamese twins, that most people find themselves drawn here. Meanwhile, Bethersden has become best known for its marble - a fossil encrusted stone - that can be found in the building work of Kent's two cathedrals and numerous parish churches.

Vineyards, Biddenden

Situated at the northern edge of the marshland lies Folkestone, a small and ancient fishing village that, after the arrival of the railway in 1842, developed into a fashionable seaside resort. From here, in the 19th century, ships ferried passengers across the Channel but, today, it is trains, onto which vehicles are loaded, that take holidaymakers to France through the Channel Tunnel. To the south are the delightful former ports of Hythe, Dymchurch and New Romney that were linked in the 1920s by the charming and much loved Romney Hythe and Dymchurch Railway. Built for an eccentric millionaire racing driver to one third scale, this railway, though its has been more popular, is still a much loved attraction that carries passengers down the coast to Dungeness.

Finally there are the remote and isolated marshes that are protected from the sea by the Dymchurch Wall and by the Royal Military Canal and an old cliff line. Once a bay of the sea, draining and reclamation of the land began as long ago as Roman times and today it is an area of rich farmland and the home of the hardy Romney sheep. This was, too, the preserve of smugglers who hid their ill-gotten gains in drainage ditches, isolated farm buildings and even churches.

WOODLANDS AND MARSHES

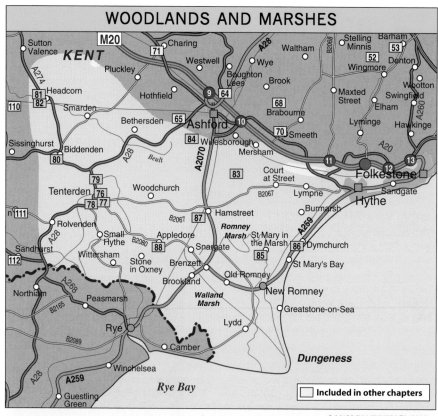

© MAPS IN MINUTES ™ (2000)

PLACES TO STAY, EAT, DRINK AND SHOP

TENTERDEN

Often referred to as the 'Jewel of the Weald', despite being situated right on the border between the dense woodlands of the Weald and the flatter farmland that leads eastwards to Romney Marsh, Tenterden is a charming town of considerable age. Today's well earned

Tenterden

nickname is, however, a far cry from its earliest days when it was known as 'Tenet-ware-den' or 'pig pasture of the men of Thanet'! Although pigs certainly did flourished here and in the surrounding area, sheep inevitably became the more profitable animal to farm these fertile lands and the wool trade quickly began to grow and the town develop. In 1331, the far sighted Edward III prohibited the export of unwashed wool and encouraged weavers from Flanders to settle here and bring their dyeing and weaving techniques to England. The town prospered and became one of the most important centres for the manufacture of broadcloth during the Middle Ages. However, in the 16th century, the fortunes of the clothiers were altered by an act of Parliament and the wool trade began to decline. There are still buildings in the town that were built with the proceeds of the wool trade, along with elegant 18th century houses that were constructed during Tenterden's days as an agricultural market place serving the surrounding towns and villages.

The **Church of St Mildred**, in the heart of Tenterden, dates from 1180 and its most interesting feature is its unusual twin doors at the western end. Meanwhile, from the top of its 15th century tower - some 125 feet above the town - there are panoramic views out across the Weald and to the Channel coast. Another place of prayer, a Unitarian chapel that was built in 1695, is particularly interesting as this is where, in 1783, Dr Benjamin Franklin, the American statesman, philosopher and scientist,

TENTERDEN AND DISTRICT MUSEUM

Station Road, Tenterden, Kent TN30 6HN
Tel: 01580 764310 website: www.ukpages.net/kent/museum.htm

Lying close to the town's steam railway, **Tenterden and District Museum** is housed in an interesting 19th century weatherboarded building that was originally a coach house and stables. Comprising of six rooms, on two floors, the museum's collections here are both extensive and diverse and include artefacts ranging from a 1500 BC flint axe head to a recreation of a typical Victorian kitchen. Covering all aspects of Tenterden's social, commercial and agricultural history, a recent addition has been the exhibition of items found by the Channel 4 *Time Team* who excavated a site nearby and were able to confirm that ships had been built there for the medieval Royal navy.

THE WHISTLE STOP CAFÉ

2 Coombe Lane, Tenterden, Kent TN30 6AD
Tel: 01580 765450

The Whistle Stop Café takes its name from the working steam train situated a couple of hundred yards away. This popular tea room makes an ideal stop for a substantial meal. Proprietor Annie Oliver-Wanstall trained at catering college and has worked in a variety of hotels and pubs. The decor is bright and welcoming - the walls of the two adjoining rooms are decorated with a delightful mix of plain and patterned ceramic plates - and with comfortable seating for 40 the atmosphere is intimate and cosy. There is also an outdoor patio that is perfect for the summer.

Annie offers all manner of home-made cakes to accompany the wide range of hot drinks and traditional cream teas with home-made scones are an special afternoon treat here. In addition there is a chance to sample the all day breakfast (egg, bacon, sausage, tomatoes, beans, mushrooms, tea and toast) which will satisfy the hungriest of diners or a lunchtime choice of soups, salads and jacket potatoes. The excellent range of sandwiches is both imaginative and extensive and, in particular, there is a hot stilton baguette that is a very popular choice. The dessert menu includes mouth-watering treacle pudding, spotted dick, caramel apple flan and toasted Mars bars with bananas. In addition the specials board changes daily and all the dishes served at The Whistle Stop are home-cooked and freshly prepared. For tempting traditional meals with excellent service and a charming and cosy atmosphere this café is just the place.

THE VINE INN

76 High Street, Tenterden, Kent TN30 6AU
Tel: 01580 762922

Found along Tenterden's broad High Street, **The Vine Inn** is easy to pick out amongst the many late 18th century buildings as, not only is it a fine Georgian building, but it is also painted a rich cream. Originally a brewery, this splendid inn is now a popular and inviting town centre pub that continues to offer its customers, both locals and visitors alike, the very best in hospitality. Licensees, Ernie and Ali, are both friendly and welcoming and since coming here they have certainly put the inn on the map. A well known venue in and around Tenterden, with various local clubs meeting here on a regular basis, The Vine Inn is a comfortable and relaxed inn at any time. From the bar customers can choose from a wide variety of drinks that include the award winning brews from Britain's oldest brewer - Shepherd Neame.

Food too is an important aspect of life at this inn and the delicious and extensive menu, served at both lunchtime and in the evening, is sure to appeal to everyone. All the tempting dishes are home-made and, in particular, there is the chef's popular meat pie and a good selection of fresh fish. A cosy inn with roaring fires in the rustic style bar during the winter, the inn also has a secluded garden to the rear where not only are there barbecues in the summer but also an outside bar. Finally, The Vine Inn has two charming en suite guest rooms that are ideal for anyone wishing to explore further both the delights of this inn and the town.

worshipped. As an apprentice typesetter in his brother's newspaper, Franklin came to England to work in a British printing office for 18 months before returning home to set up his own newspaper. Later, and then acting as an agent for several American provinces, he moved back to England for 18 years when also, as a result of his experiments with electricity and his invention of the lightning conductor, he was elected a Fellow of the Royal Society.

Kent and East Sussex Railway

For a real insight into the history of the town and the local area a visit to the **Tenterden and District Museum** is well worth while. The displays here cover over 1,000 years of history and they relate to hop-picking, farming, the area of the Weald, the Cinque Ports and Victorian domestic life (see panel on page 107).

Tenterden is also the home of the **Kent and East Sussex Railway** that runs between the town and Northiam just over the county border in East Sussex. When the railway opened in 1900 it was the first full size light railway in the world and it quickly gained a reputation for its distinctive and charming atmosphere that

it still retains today. Travelling through glorious, unspoilt countryside, that will be familiar to anyone who saw the television series *The Darling Buds of May*, passengers journey in beautifully restored carriages that date from Victorian times up until the 1960s and they are pulled by one of the railway's dozen steam locomotives. Adjacent to the station at Tenterden is the **Colonel Stephens' Railway Museum** where the fascinating story of the Colonel, who built and ran this railway along with several other independent lines, is told.

AROUND TENTERDEN

SMARDEN
5½ miles N of Tenterden off the A262

This ancient Wealden market town's name comes from a Saxon word meaning 'butter valley and pasture' and this charming place has managed to keep its original character along with some beautiful old half-timbered cottages and houses set along the single main street. A centre for the

Kent and East Sussex Railway

LITTLE SILVER COUNTRY HOTEL

Ashford Road, St Michael's, Tenterden, Kent TN30 6SP
Tel: 01233 850321 Fax: 01233 850647
e-mail: enquiries@little-silver.co.uk
website: www.little-silver.co.uk

Set within its own beautifully landscaped grounds in the heart of the Weald of Kent, **Little Silver Country Hotel** is a small and intimate establishment that offers guests a personal and friendly service. Owned and personally run by Christine and Oliver Johnston, with the help of their friendly Golden Labrador Shasta and George, a silver tabby, this elegant Tudor-style establishment has the feel and atmosphere of a family home rather than a hotel. The spacious oak beamed lounge, where an open fire blazes during the winter, is furnished with plenty of large, comfortable armchairs that are perfect for settling down in with a good book. Meanwhile, the cosy cocktail bar is just the place to enjoy a pre or post dinner drink in elegant surroundings.

Whilst breakfast is served in a Victorian style conservatory overlooking the gardens, dinner is taken in the more formal surroundings of the dining room where crisp table linen, candles and gleaming silverware add to the sense of occasion. The excellent menu of modern European cuisine changes regularly and dinner here is complemented by an equally superb wine list. Each of

the 10 en suite guest rooms has been individually furnished and decorated and whilst some have four poster beds others have Jacuzzi baths. However, all the rooms share the same attention to detail in the manner of the facilities provided that all help to ensure that staying here is a pleasant and relaxing experience. Although the hotel is superb, it would be a great mistake not to venture out and explore the gardens as they are as impressive as the house. Not surprisingly, Little Silver Country Hotel has become a popular venue for wedding receptions and, away from the hotel's main buildings, is the magnificent Kent Hall where such celebrations can be held in their own self-contained oast house style building. Throughout the year, Christine and Oliver offer special breaks and dogs can be taken by prior arrangement.

Cottage, Smarden

cloth industry in the Middle Ages, the village's 14th century church has become known as the 'Barn of Kent' because of its huge roof.

BETHERSDEN
5 miles NE of Tenterden on the A28

This small village has long been associated with its 'marble' that was quarried in medieval times and used in many of Kent's churches and its two cathedrals. Calling the stone 'marble' is a little misleading as it is actually a type of fossil encrusted stone. Although the village is situated on the main Tenterden to Ashford road and had an abundance of local building materials such as its famous stone, Bethersden was considered, in the 18th century, to have some of the worst roads in Kent.

WOODCHURCH
4 miles E of Tenterden off the B2067

In the heart of this large village lies the green around which are grouped several charming typically Kentish houses - including one dating back to Tudor times and others from the Georgian period. It was on this green, in 1826, that a battle

took place between a smuggling gang and the Dragoons. The gang members were caught, tried, sentenced and then transported to Australia.

One of the fine buildings to be found here is **Woodchurch Windmill**, an impressive white smock mill that was constructed in 1820. Fully renovated and with its original machinery restored to full working order, the mill also houses a display of photographs that tell of its history and illustrate the restoration work. From the mill there are spectacular views over the marshes to the Channel coast.

Also found at Woodchurch is the **South of England Rare Breeds Centre** that, as its name might suggest, is home to a large collection of rare British farm breeds, such as the Lincoln Longwool sheep that date back to Roman times and the Bagot goat that was brought to Britain by the Crusaders. Young visitors can meet many of the centre's animals in the Children's Barn and there are trailer rides and woodland walks to enjoy.

SMALL HYTHE
2 miles S of Tenterden on the B2082

Hard though it might be to imagine today but this little hamlet was once a flourishing port and shipbuilding centre. In the Middle Ages, the River Rother flowed past Small Hythe and it was both wide enough and deep enough to accommodate the ships of those days and one of Henry VIII's warships was built here. Today, there is little trace of this village's past life or, indeed, of the river as, even in the wettest weather, it is little more than a tiny stream. One clue,

Half Timbered House, Small Hythe

being the home of the famous Shakespearean actress Ellen Terry. Living here between 1899 and 1928, the house, that is now in the ownership of the National Trust, contains many of her personal items, including some of her stage costumes and numerous artefacts relating to other great thespians. Meanwhile, the house itself still contains many of its original features and, outside, there is a delightful cottage garden and an Elizabethan barn that was adapted into a theatre in the late 1920s.

however, to those long ago days lies in the name of the Small Hythe bus stop that is called the Ferry.

Close to the village lies **Smallhythe Place** a charming 16th century half-timbered house that is best known for

Small Hythe is also the home of **Tenterden Vineyard** where visitors can walk around the growing vines, tour the herb garden, take in the rural museum and enjoy refreshments at the tea room

YE MAYDES RESTAURANT

High Street, Biddenden,
Kent TN27 8AR
Tel: 01580 291306
Fax: 01580 292064

Housed in a wonderful Grade I listed building, that dates from around 1500 and that also has connections with Flemish weavers, **Ye Maydes Restaurant** is a place that is well worth finding. Owner, Sheila Daniels, has been here for nearly 30 years and, with the assistance of chef Julie, they have developed a very loyal local following.

The exceptionally well preserved exterior prepares customers for the olde worlde interior with its heavily beamed ceilings and inviting fires burning in the grates of the inglenook fireplaces. However, this is also a very comfortable restaurant where great attention has been paid to detail. Nowhere, though, is this more apparent than on the menus where a tantalising list of mouth-watering dishes is sure to tempt even the most jaded of palates. A subtle blend of English and French cuisine, the menus change regularly and make not only interesting reading but also making a choice difficult. A place that combines the very best cuisine with a friendly service and an outstanding medieval setting, Ye Maydes Restaurant is certainly worth travelling to enjoy.

before picking up a memento at the vineyard's gift shop.

WITTERSHAM
4 miles S of Tenterden on the B2082

Situated high above the Rother Levels, some 200 feet above sea level, and right in the middle of the Isle of Oxney, Wittersham has been given the affectionate title of the 'Capital of the Isle' despite being not significantly larger, or more important, than many of the area's other villages. The skeleton of a prehistoric iguanadon was uncovered here and, more recently, Wittersham was a mooring site for airships during World War I. Nearby, lies **Stocks Mill**, the tallest post mill in Kent, that was erected on this site in 1781 and restored by the County Council in 1980.

BIDDENDEN
4 miles NW of Tenterden on the A262

Well recognised as one of the finest villages in the Weald of Kent, Biddenden has an attractive main street that is lined with charming half-timbered houses. Ranging from medieval times through to the 17th century, there are many fine examples of period architecture and also some interesting old weaver's houses - situated on the south side of the street to make the most of the available light - that date back to the time when this was a centre of the cloth trade. Now converted into shops, above the door of one of these old houses is a carved head that is said to have come from a Spanish ship that was wrecked during the Armada.

At the western end of the main street stands **All Saints'**

Church that was founded by the Saxons but, of the present building, the oldest parts remaining, such as the nave, chancel and south aisle, date from the 13th century. The tower, that was funded by the thriving cloth trade, was erected in 1400 and it is made from Bethersden marble.

Although this is undoubtedly a delightful place to visit with some fine buildings to see it is the **Biddenden Maids** that arouse most visitors curiosity. Born in Biddenden in 1100, Eliza and Mary Chulkhurst were Siamese twins who, despite being joined at both the hip and shoulders, lived to be 34 years old. A rare occurrence today, the birth of these special twins was an occasion of unheralded novelty in a medieval community and this has earned them a permanent place in the history books. Local legend has it that, when one of the sisters died the other refused to be separated from her twin, saying, "As we

Biddenden

FOUR OAKS

Four Oaks Road, Headcorn, Kent TN27 9PB
Tel: 01622 891224 Fax: 01622 890630
e-mail: info@fouroaks.uk.com
website: fouroaks.uk.com

Situated in its own large and well tendered gardens, **Four Oaks** is a beautiful, half weatherboarded, 500 year old farmhouse that has been fully restored and, although it now has a peg tile roof, it was probably originally thatched. The addition of an extension, that is very much in keeping with the style of the house, has made this into a wonderfully spacious dwelling without the loss of the intimacy of a family home. Rosanne and Richard Thick have been living here some 15 years and, since 1998, they have been offering superb bed and breakfast accommodation. Each of the three guest rooms is, like the rest of the house, tastefully decorated and furnished and, as well as the excellent facilities, they all have

features that mirror the age and style of the house. Downstairs is the combined dining room and lounge where guests are treated to a delicious breakfast and, by arrangement, an evening meal.

Very much part of the family house, there are family photographs on display, guests will find that this is just the place to rest in front of the large log fire and enjoy a glass of wine and a chat with their hosts and other guests. Meanwhile, the garden is also well worth exploring and, to the front, is a large pond, complete with ducks and fish that is sure to charm children.

THE KING'S ARMS

1-3 High Street, Headcorn, Kent TN27 9NH
Tel: 01622 890216

Found in the centre of the village, and opposite the original coach house where the archway can still be seen, is **The King's Arms**. Dating back to the early 16th cneutry and probably originating as an ale house, this delightful inn continues to provide warm and friendly hospitality to all its customers. Before becoming the licensees here in summer 2000, Ann and Gordon had worked here and their experience along with their popularity has gone to add further to the excellent reputation of the inn.

Very much a locals meeting place, particularly in winter when there are few holidaymakers around,

The King's Arms not only has a well stocked bar but there is also a good menu of traditional home-cooked dishes, such as steak and kidney pie and lamb stew, available every lunchtime and most evenings and a popular roast lunch on Sundays. Add to this the comfortable bed and breakfast accommodation, the secluded rear beer garden and the regular live music and it is easy to see why this inn is so well frequented.

came together we will also go together", and she died some six hours later. Although the twins, obviously, had problems of their own they bequested some land for the poor and needy of Biddenden that is still generating money today.

HEADCORN
7½ miles NW of Tenterden on the A274

This is another of the charming and ancient Wealden villages that litter this area of the county and, as with many of its neighbours, Headcorn too was a thriving centre of cloth manufacturing. One still visible result of this wealth are the many fine buildings to be seen here, including **Shakespeare House** and **The Chequers** that are both excellent examples of Elizabethan timbered buildings. Beyond the large 14th century church that was constructed using local Bethersden marble, lies a magnificent hall house that has changed little since it was erected some 600 years ago. Despite all this antiquity, Headcorn is also a modern village and it provides shopping facilities for the smaller surrounding communities.

Just to the south of the village, at **Lashenden**, is the **Lashenden Air Warfare Museum** that commemorates the role played by this area of Kent during World War II and the Battle of Britain in particular. On display are numerous wartime exhibits, from both Britain and Germany, including a piloted V1 flying bomb, ration books and many photographs.

FOLKESTONE

A port and small fishing village since Saxon times, it was the arrival of the South Eastern railway in 1842 that transformed Folkestone into the major port and elegant resort that it is today. Within a year of the first passenger train service running, passenger ships had started to ferry people across the English Channel to Boulogne and, even then, the journey time from London to Paris was just 12 hours. Much of the town dates from the Victorian age whilst the wide avenues and formal gardens remain a legacy of the elegant Edwardian era. What is most unusual about this particular seaside resort, however, is that it does not have a recognisable seafront but, instead, it has **The Leas**, a wide and sweeping promenade with a series of delightful clifftop lawns and flower gardens, that has a distinctly Mediterranean feel.

Oast Houses, Headcorn

Folkestone Harbour

The name comes from a Kent dialect word meaning an open space. Meanwhile, the **Leas Cliff Lift**, the oldest water-balanced lift in the country, carries people from the clifftops to the beach below. Not far from the lower lift entrance lies **The Rotunda Fun Park**, with its traditional seaside amusements, that provides attractions for all the family.

Throughout all this development in the late 19th and early 20th century Folkestone has managed to retain its original ancient fishing village and this is concentrated in an area known as **The Lanterns**. One of the oldest buildings in the town is its parish **Church of St Mary and St Eanswythe** that dates back to the 13th century. St Eanswythe was a Kent princess who founded a nunnery in what is now Folkestone in the 7th century and, whilst her bones are buried here, the church also remembers the town's most famous son, William Harvey, in its west window. Born in Church Street, a part of the town that was home to traders of cloth and silk, in 1578, Harvey was a physician to both James I and Charles I but he is best remembered for his discovery of the circulation of blood in the human body. Unfortunately, it would seem that all of Harvey's medical skills counted for nothing when it came to his

own fate for he is reputed to have committed suicide in 1657 after discovering that he was going blind.

The story of the town, from its Saxon roots right through to the present day, is told at the **Folkestone Museum** and the numerous displays and exhibits here range from the early traders, the growth of the medieval port and the town as a smugglers' haven to its development into a fashionable resort. The geology of this corner of Kent is also explored and, hundreds of millions of years ago, this area was deep under a tropical sea. Meanwhile, at **Martello Tower No 3**, one of numerous such towers that were built as a defence against the possible invasion of the country by Napoleon, there is an exhibition that illustrates the measures taken to defend the south coast.

As long ago as the early 19th century, when a French engineer presented Napoleon with plans for a tunnel linking France and England, the idea of such a thoroughfare, then designed for horse-drawn carriages, has captured the imagination. So much so, in fact, that, in 1877, a tunnel was started, from both sides, but work on this ceased, almost before it had begun, because of the public outcry in England. However, in 1986, work on the present Channel Tunnel began and, now complete, Folkestone is the English home of the **Channel Tunnel Terminal** where both passenger cars and freight lorries join the trains that take them under the Channel to continental Europe.

A far cry from the bustle associated with the tunnel terminal, **The Folkestone Warren** is a peaceful country park that provides a habitat for numerous birds, insects and small mammals. The clifftop grasslands that were once grazed by sheep and cattle have now been colonised by, in some cases, rare wild flowers while there are also the beautiful plants, such as Wild Cabbage and Rock Samphire, that grow on the chalk cliffs.

AROUND FOLKESTONE

SANDGATE
1 mile SW of Folkestone on the A259

Now more a suburb of Folkestone that a village in its own right, Sandgate is a haven for collectors as its main street is littered with interesting and differing antique shops. This is a peaceful place now but, during the threat of an invasion by Napoleon, no less that six Martello Towers were built in the area and these impressive granite structures overlook the village.

In 1898 and aged 32, the by then famous author HG Wells moved to Sandgate and, on the proceeds of his successful novels, he moved into Spade House, in 1900, that had been specially designed for him by CF Voysey. Situated at the foot of Sandgate Hill, it was here that he entertained his literary friends and continued to write articles and papers advocating social and political change as well as more successful novels. Spade House is not open to the public.

HYTHE
4 miles W of Folkestone on the A259

The recorded history of Hythe goes back to AD 732 when Elthelred, King of the Saxons, first granted it a charter and

its name, which means 'landing place', refers to the time when there was a busy harbour here and Hythe played an important role as one of the Cinque Ports. However, decline set in as the harbour began to silt up and today this historic town not only lies half a mile from the sea but also no sign of its harbour remains.

Hythe is a delightful and ancient town to visit that has plenty to offer visitors, particularly those interested in beautiful old buildings. The skyline is dominated by the Norman tower of **St Leonard's Church** that was built in 1080 and that, along with several interesting features, has a **Crypt** where over 2,000 skulls (and various other assorted human bones that date back to before the Norman invasion) are on display. For more information on the history of Hythe, the **Hythe Local History Room** is the ideal place to visit. This fascinating museum not only has numerous artefacts on display but also a model of the town dated 1907.

Today, this charming place is best known as being one of the terminals for the **Romney Hythe and Dymchurch Railway**, that offers passengers a 14 mile journey, by steam train, across the edge of Romney Marsh to Dungeness.

Hythe Beach

A mile to the north of Hythe lies **Saltwood Castle** that, whilst not open to the public, can be seen from a nearby bridleway. It was once the residence of the Archbishop of Canterbury and it was here that Becket's murderers stayed whilst journeying from France to commit their evil act. More recently, Lord Clark, the famous art historian and presenter of the pioneering television series *Civilisation* made this his home when he purchased the estate from Bill Deedes, the veteran journalist. After his death his son, Alan Clark, the glamorous Member of Parliament, lived here until 1999 when he, too, died.

LYMPNE
2½ miles W of Folkestone off the B2067

Pronounced 'Limm', Lympne was established by the Romans as a port, known as Portus Lemanis, and, in the 3rd century, they built a fort here. Now standing on the site of this ancient fort is **Lympne Castle**, a fortified manor house that has both Norman towers as well as medieval architectural features. From here there are glorious panoramic views out across Romney Marsh, along the line of the Royal Military Canal and down the coast to Dungeness.

Just beyond the castle lies **Port Lympne Wild Animal Park** that was created by John Aspinall and shares the same aim, of the preserving of rare and endangered species, as its sister park Howletts. The large wild animal wilderness is home to many animals, including Indian elephants, tigers, lions, gorillas and monkeys, and also the largest captive group of black rhino in the world. After taking a safari trailer ride around the park, visitors have the opportunity to discover the delights of the park's historic mansion house that was built by Sir Philip Sassoon, MP, in 1915. In particular, the house is

The Black Rabbit

Frith Road, Aldington Frith, Kent TN25 7HQ
Tel: 01233 720426 Fax: 01233 721330

The Black Rabbit is a well hidden place, but well worth seeking out if you are in the area and looking for some fine food and drink. If you head for the village of Aldington, just off the A20, then take the Frith road back towards Ashford you should stumble across it soon enough - otherwise just ring! The corner location makes The Black Rabbit quite prominent, so you are unlikely to drive straight past it.

Once you have arrived then you will quickly discover how friendly the staff are, and how comfortable and welcoming the interior. There are plenty of tables and chairs, with lots of little alcoves and corners in which to tuck yourself away if you wish.

A freehouse, the bar stocks a varied selection of popular real ales, beer and lager, though it really is the food that most people come here for. The menu is impressively wide ranging, offering much more

varied dishes than you would normally find in a pub. There are some traditional English dishes but there is a strong Continental feel together with a large selection of Tex-Mex dishes which prove to be exceedingly popular. Food is served every day at lunch (except Mondays, unless a Bank Holiday) and in the evening with a special two meals for the price of one on a Monday, Pizza Specials on a Wednesday and roasts at Sunday lunch. Booking ahead is strongly advised. There are also regular theme nights, such as Mediaeval Banquets, ring for details of what is coming up when you're in the area.

home to the Spencer Roberts Animal Mural Room, where the walls are covered with colourful paintings of the exotic animals, whilst, outside, there are beautiful landscaped gardens.

COURT-AT-STREET
4 miles W of Folkestone on the B2067

The ruined chapel here is connected with the tragic tale of the Holy Maid of Kent, Elizabeth Arton who, in 1525, claimed that she had direct communication with the Mother of God. Her pronouncements made her famous and she was persuaded to enter a convent at Canterbury by clergy seeking to capitalise financially on the increasing public interest in her powers. However, in 1533 Elizabeth made the mistake of suggesting that Henry VIII would died if he divorced his first wife, Queen Catherine, and married Anne Boleyn and she (along with those clerics who had faith in her) was hanged at Tyburn in 1534.

THE QUEENS HEAD
Ashford Road, Kingsnorth, near Ashford, Kent TN23 3ED
Tel: 01233 620769

Standing on the main road through this pretty country village, **The Queens Head** is a lovely old building that is hard to miss. Originally the home of a blacksmith's forge, this delightful inn is a popular place that is well known for its warm and friendly atmosphere. Landlord, Derek Holland,

grew up on the Kent coast, at Dover, and, at The Queens Head, he has created the perfect place in which to relax.

Because of its previous life as a forge, the interior of this charming inn is made up of a series of small rooms that provide intimate hideaways whilst the main bar is large and more spacious - ideal for a get together. Cosy, inviting and just the place to escape from the winter weather, in the summer customers spill out of the inn into the large, rear beer garden where there is always a glorious display of colourful, flower filled hanging baskets and patio tubs.

However, whatever the time of year the high standard of the hospitality at The Queens Head is maintained. The real ales served here have all been specially chosen for their taste and quality whilst non beer drinkers will find that the bar offers a wide choice of all the usual drinks. Food, too, features highly at The Queens Head and the inn is well known locally for its superb, home-cooked menus that range from tasty sandwiches to traditional pub dishes and there is a popular roast lunch served on Sundays. In particular, the starters show considerable flair and imagination and they provide an exciting beginning to a delicious meal. Meanwhile, there is a small, select wine list to further add to customers' dining experience. Visitors should also look out for the inn's occasional themed evenings.

MERSHAM
10 miles NW of Folkestone off the A20

To the southwest of this village lies **Swanton Mill**, a charming old rural watermill powered by the River East Stour that is surrounded by a beautiful garden. The restoration work undertaken on the mill has won awards and, today, the mill is still working and produces wholemeal flour.

NEW ROMNEY

Known as the 'Capital of the Marsh', New Romney is an attractive old town with some fine Georgian houses, that was, at one time, the most important of the Cinque Ports. However, in 1287 a great storm choked the River Rother, on which the town stood, with shingle and caused the river's course to be diverted to Rye. The town lost its harbour and its status, although the Cinque Port documents are still housed at the guildhall, and New Romney now lies a mile from the sea. The sole survivor of the four churches in the town that were recorded in the Domesday Book, **St Nicholas' Church** still dominates the town's skyline with its 100 foot high west tower. However, of more interest to most visitors are the floodmarks that can be seen on the pillars inside the church that indicate just how high the floodwaters rose in late 13th century.

The town is best known as being home to the main station of the **Romney Hythe and Dymchurch Railway**, a charming one third scale railway that was built in the 1920s for the millionaire racing driver, Captain Howey. Opened in 1927 as the 'World's Smallest Public Railway', and running between Hythe and Dungeness, it was not uncommon for train loads of holidaymakers to find that their carriages

THE STAR INN

St Mary in the Marsh, Kent TN29 0BX Tel: 01797 362139
e-mail: marc@star-inn-the-marsh.co.uk website: www.star-inn-the-marsh.co.uk

Found in the middle of the Romney Marsh, and adjacent to the house where Noel Coward lived as a young boy, **The Star Inn** is a charming old free house that dates back to 1476 - the same year that William Caxton set up his printing press. Originally a row of thatched farm cottages, this was a well established free house by the 19th century when, during lambing time, the inn's fires were continuously lit so that shepherds could find warm shelter here throughout the day and night. Hosts, Marc and Jenny van Overstraeten are just as welcoming today and, since they first came here in 1983, they have established The Star as a friendly and inviting inn that offers superb food, drink and accommodation. The real ales served from bar change with the seasons and many unusual brews are featured. Jenny is

responsible for the cooking and, whilst her steak and kidney pie is very much a pub favourite, the menu also includes such tasty delights as lamb ragout, tipsy beef casserole, game, fish and lighter snacks. During the winter, the roaring fire adds an extra glow in this very traditional and unspoilt old inn whilst, outside, on warmer days customers can enjoy the extensive beer garden with its outlook over the marsh. A delightful and charming inn where those taking advantage of the excellent bed and breakfast accommodation can truly experience the relaxed and comfortable nature of this inn.

were being pulled by a locomotive driven by a famous friend of the Captain. During World War II, the railway was run by the army who used it move both troops and supplies along this stretch of the south coast. Although revived in the post war boom years, the railway struggled to attract visitors in the 1960s but it was, fortunately, saved by a group of enthusiastic businessmen. Whilst not necessarily as popular today as it has been, the railway is still a delightful way to explore this coastline and it makes a fascinating day out for all the family. Meanwhile, at the New Romney station can be found the **Romney Toy and Model Museum** that houses a wonderful collection of old and not so old toys, dolls, models, posters and photographs. There are also two magnificent working model railways that are sure to captivate children of all ages.

St Mary's Bay

AROUND NEW ROMNEY

ST MARY IN THE MARSH
2 miles N of New Romney off the A259

Set on the lonely and remote flats of Romney Marsh, this village's church steeple is crowned by an interesting ball and weather vane, the ball of which was obviously used by the villagers for target practice as, during restoration work, honey, from the bees who had made their hive in the ball, was found to be oozing from the bullet holes. Meanwhile, in the churchyard lies the simple grave of E Nesbit, the author of children's books whose most famous novel is *The Railway Children*.

DYMCHURCH
3½ miles NE of New Romney on the A259

This small town's name is derived from 'Deme' the medieval English word

meaning judge or arbiter and the town was the home of the governors of Romney Marsh. Known as the Lords of the Level, it was these men who saw that swift justice was carried out on anyone endangering the well being of marshes and they still meet today. Visitors can find out more about the history of Romney Marsh at the **Lords of the Level**, a small museum housed in the town's old courtroom.

At one time a quiet and secluded village, Dymchurch has become a busy seaside resort with a five mile stretch of sandy beach and all the usual amusements arcades, giftshops and cafés. However, what does make it rather different from other such resorts is the **Dymchurch Wall**, a sea wall that prevents water from flooding both the town and marsh as Dymchurch lies about seven and a half feet below the level of the high tide. A barrier has existed here since Roman times.

Visitors can go from one formidable defence to another at Dymchurch as the **Martello Tower** here is, arguably, the best example of its kind in the country. Now fully restored and with its original 24 pounder gun, complete with traversing carriage, still on the roof, this is one of the 74 such towers that were built along the coast as protection against invasion by Napoleon. Their name is derived from their 'pepper-pot' shape as they are similar in style to a tower that stood at Cape Mortella in Corsica. This was an ironic choice of model as Napoleon himself was born on that Mediterranean island.

From the 1890s onwards the children's author, Edith Nesbit (but always E Nesbit on her novels), came to Dymchurch and other places around Romney Marsh to work on her novels. As well as writing she would explore the marshland churches, riding first on a bicycle and later in a dog cart, before finally moving to Jesson St Mary where she spent her last years.

THE CHANTRY HOUSE

21 Sycamore Gardens, Dymchurch, Kent TN29 0LS
Tel: 01303 873137 Fax: 01303 873137

Found close to the sea in peaceful and secluded surroundings, **The Chantry House** is a charming hotel that is so called as it was originally a home for the monks from the church opposite. Although parts of the building date back to the 18th century, it is essentially a Victorian house and that is now provides superb accommodation with a relaxed and quiet atmosphere. Owners Anne and Steve Dartnall have been at this family run hotel since 1997 and, in time, they have gained a reputation for offering excellent hospitality for all the family, including both children and the family dog. There are seven comfortable en suite guest rooms here, some with four poster beds and other with views out over the sea.

Dining here is a real treat as the restaurant offers a full à la carte menu that includes locally caught fish, game when in season and the house speciality, home-made pies. Delicious cream teas are also

served in the afternoon. Those looking around the hotel will not fail to miss the many interesting military artefacts, including guns and medals, that are on show. However, by fare the most impressive item of militaria can be found outside. The pride of the collection of a 1943 Russian T34 battle tank that was built by Russian women and that was, along with the harsh Russian winter, responsible for the destruction of the German army on the eastern front. From the garden too is a private entrance to the sandy beach via a footbridge to the sea wall.

BURMARSH
5 miles NE of New Romney off the A259

Found at the northern end of Romney Marsh, this village is home to one of the area's marshland churches, All Saints' Church, that boasts an impressive Norman doorway that is crowned by a grotesque man's face. Two of the original late 14th century bells are still rung today whilst another, dedicated to Magdalene, has been preserved. At nearby **Lathe Barn**, children get the opportunity to meet and befriend a whole range of farm animals including ducks, chicks, barn owls, rabbits, donkeys calves and sheep.

DUNGENESS
5 miles S of New Romney off the B2075

This southern most corner of Kent, with its shingle beach, has been a treacherous headland that has been feared by sailors for centuries. Originally simple fires were lit on the beach to warn shipping of the dangers around this headland and, in 1615, the first proper lighthouse was erected. As the sea has retreated a succession of lighthouses have been built and today there are now two at Dungeness. The **Old Lighthouse** that dates from 1901 and its modern and current successor, Lighthouse number five, that was opened in 1961. From the top of the Old Lighthouse, after a climb of 169 steps, there are glorious views out to sea and, inland, over the marshes. As well as the makeshift fishermen's shacks, and the lighthouses, the other key building on the headland is **Dungeness Power Station** where, at the **Visitor Centre**, there is an exhibition on electricity and the generation of nuclear energy. Guided tours of the power station can also be taken. The headland is also home to the **Dungeness Nature Reserve** whose flat lands have been described as "the last natural undisturbed area in the South East and larger than any similar stretch of land in Europe." This RSPB reserve is noted for the many rare and migrating birds that come here to rest and feed and it is a haven for lovers of wildfowl.

LYDD
3 miles SE of New Romney on the B2076

Like Old Romney, Lydd was once a busy port, linked to the Cinque Port of New Romney, but the changing of the course of the River Rother and the steady build up of land along the marsh put paid to this. Despite the loss of the port trade and now lying some three miles from the sea, Lydd is still an attractive place that has retained many mementoes of its more prosperous past. Along with some fine merchants' houses and the handsome guildhall, the town is home to one of the tallest and longest parish churches in Kent, the 13th century **All Saints' Church** that is often referred to as the 'Cathedral of the Marsh'. Whilst the church was being restored following bomb damage it sustained in 1940, a stone altar that had been thrown out by Reformers was rediscovered and it now stands in the north chancel. Before his meteoric rise to fame, Cardinal Wolsey was the rector of Lydd in 1503.

Housed in the old fire station, **Lydd Town Museum** has a fascinating collection of memorabilia on the history of the town and local area along with a Merryweather fire engine and an early 20th century horsebus. Meanwhile, at Lydd Library, the **Romney Marsh Craft Gallery** has a permanent display of crafts from both Romney Marsh and further afield that can be purchased.

OLD ROMNEY
2 miles W of New Romney on the A259

With its setting in the remote Romney Marsh, this tiny village has a forlorn feel and it is hard to imagine that this place was once a prosperous port. However, the

Domesday Book records that Old Romney had three fisheries, a mill and a wharf, thereby indicating that it had a waterfront. As the marsh gained more land from the sea, Romney's position - which had been as a busy island - became landlocked and trading became seriously hampered. So Old Romney lost out to New Romney that ironically also found itself victim of the gradually accretion of land in the marsh.

Just its name, **Romney Marsh**, is enough to conjure up images of smugglers lugging their contraband across the misty marshland and, for centuries, this whole area profited from the illegal trade that was known locally as 'owling' because of the coded calls the smugglers used in order to avoid the excise men. Whilst Rudyard Kipling has painted a charming and romantic picture of the marsh in his poetry, another writer, Russell Thorndyke, told of a rougher side in his children's

novel, *Dr Syn*, that was published in 1915. As well as being the vicar of Dymchurch, Dr Syn was the leader of a gang of smugglers in the 18th century who killed excise men, fought battles with the militia and stored their contraband in the marshland churches.

BROOKLAND
4½ miles W of New Romney on the A259

Brookland certainly has a name that describes its setting - on the southern fringes of Romney Marsh where the landscape is one of flooded meadows, small ditches and dykes. Despite its location, the village is home to an impressive church, that of St Augustine, that is said to be built from the timber of local shipwrecks. Whilst, inside, the church has some fine features - such as the medieval wall painting of the murder of Thomas à Becket and a cylindrical lead Norman font that is unique in Britain - it

WORLD'S WONDER

Warehorne, Nr. Ashford, Kent TN26 2LU
Tel: 01233 732431

The unusually named **World's Wonder** is a large imposing pub which can be easily found on the B2067 in the village of Warehorne, between Tenterden and Hamstreet. It is believed that the building started out as two cottages which were bought by a local man, Thomas Knight, over 140 years ago. For many months the villagers wondered what he was going to do with them, and eventually he obtained a beer license, knocked the two cottages into one large property and stopped the villagers wondering by calling it 'World's Wonder'.

Whatever the reason for its unusual name, this is a traditional country pub offering a friendly welcome to customers old and new, and serving them fine refreshment. The bar stocks at least three real ales, some from a local brewer, together with the usual lagers and Guinness also on tap. Food is served each lunch time and evening all year round, and available all day in the summer. The menu offers a good selection of traditional snacks and hot dishes catering to all tastes and appetites, supplemented by a blackboard of specials. There are occasional themed food evenings and live entertainment is arranged in the summer - ring for details.

is the church's belfry that is most interesting. Built in three vertical wooden stages, it stands quite apart from the rest of the church in much the same way that the campanile of an Italian church or cathedral is separate. Dating from the 13th century, architectural historians suspect that the medieval builders feared that the church, built on such damp foundations, would not support the extra weight of a belfry if it was added to the original building.

BRENZETT
4 miles NW of New Romney off the A259

This small settlement, that lies on the probably Roman **Rhee Wall** sea embankment, is home to one of the smallest of the marshland churches, St Eanswith's Church. Thought to have been founded in the 7th century, although no traces of this building survive, there is an interesting tomb to

local landowner John Fagge and his son to be seen here. Meanwhile, the **Brenzett Aeronautical Museum** houses a unique collection of wartime aircraft memorabilia including equipment and articles recovered from crash sites.

APPLEDORE
7 miles NW of New Romney on the A2080

Originally a port on the estuary of the River Rother, the violent storm in the 13th century, that changed the course of the river and the resultant silting up, has left Appledore some eight miles from the sea. However, this did not prevent French raiders, in 1380, arriving here and setting fire to the village's 13th century church. Later, in the early 19th century, under the threat of another invasion by the French, this time under Napoleon, the **Royal Military Canal** was built and it passes through the village. Encircling Romney Marsh, the canal's sweeping bends meant

THE SWAN HOTEL

The Street, Appledore, Kent TN26 2BU
Tel: 01233 758000

Although the present day **Swan Hotel** only dates from 1910, the inn was built on the site of a much older establishment that dated from 1689 and was an inn from 1741 onwards. Despite this solidly constructed brick inn seemingly lacking in character, from the outside, the interior is cosy and inviting with the real atmosphere of a traditional English inn that goes back for centuries. As well as the gleaming horse brasses decorating the walls, there is an interesting display of old photographs. Well known for serving a good selection of real ales, landlords Jane Homewood and Gary Ord, have also gained a reputation for serving excellent home-made pub food and for the occasional Irish nights and live music evenings that they hold.

A popular inn with both visitors and locals, that caters to all the family, including the dog, there is plenty of space outside for eating and drinking in fine weather and The Swan Hotel also offers comfortable bed and breakfast accom-modation in a choice of three well appointed guest rooms.

that the whole length of the waterway could be protected by cannon fire and it was designed as a means of quickly flooding the marshland in the event of the expected invasion. However, by the time that the canal had been completed, in 1807, the threat of invasion had ended but, during World War II, when it seemed likely that Hitler would try to land his forces on English soil, pillboxes were built along the length of the canal.

SNARGATE
5 miles NW of New Romney off the B2080

Found in the heart of the Romney Marsh, this village's remote location conjures up the days when smugglers plied their illicit trade under the cover of darkness and hid their ill-gotten gains in reed lined streams or in disused and isolated farm buildings. The 600 year old parish **Church of St Dunstan**, built in an exposed position, seems, on first impressions, to be disproportionately large for the size of this village. However, this extra space was a boon for smugglers as they used it to store their contraband. An excise raid in 1743 uncovered a cask of gin in the vestry and tobacco in the belfry! In the early 19th century the vicar here was the Rev Richard Barham and during his time at Snargate he wrote his humorous tales, the *Ingoldsby Legends*, some of which relate to the people of the marsh. As he lived at some distance from the village Barham was unaware of the night time activity centred around his church.

STONE-IN-OXNEY
8 miles NW of New Romney off the B2080

Strikingly situated on the eastern flank of the inland island known as the Isle of Oxney, the stone that gives the village its name is Roman and can be found, preserved, in the parish Church of St Mary. Other archaeological remains within the church suggest that this site once served as a temple to Mithras, a Persian deity beloved of Roman soldiers.

6 The Weald of Kent

The Weald of Kent is a name to be reckoned with and one that conjures up, quite rightly, images of rolling wooded countryside, orchards and hop fields. Cranbrook, that is often dubbed the 'Capital of the Kentish Weald', is typical of many of the towns and villages of this area. It is a charming place that prospered in the Middle Ages with the growth of the woollen trade and that, when this industry decline, reverted to being a market town serving the surrounding communities.

Further north lies Maidstone, on the River Medway that forms the border between the Kentish Men and the Men of Kent, and that, too, has an ancient history. Of the places to visit here, some of the most interesting, such as Allington Castle and the Museum of Kent Life, can be found beside this main waterway just north of the town. However, Maidstone is home to a 14th century Archbishop's Palace that was a resting place for the clergy travelling between London and Canterbury and that stands on the site of a building mentioned in the Domesday Book.

Orchards, Paddock Wood

Close to the county border with East Sussex lies Royal Tunbridge Wells, a particularly charming town that, unlike many places in the Kent, was no more than a forest clearing until the early 17th century when health restoring waters were discovered here. Developed to provide accommodation and entertainment, with the help of Beau Nash, to those coming here to take the waters, the town also received royal patronage that led to the addition of its prefix that was granted by Edward VII.

In between these key towns, the countryside its littered with attractive villages and small towns that are surrounded by the orchards and hop fields that typify the Weald. This area is also home to two of the most popular attractions in the county, if not England. Situated on two islands and surrounded by glorious gardens, the former royal palace of Leeds Castle, that was so beloved by Henry VIII, is a wonderful example of Norman defensive architecture that was thankfully restored by Lady Braillie over a period of time from 1926 onwards. Meanwhile, there is Sissinghurst Castle, the ruin that Vita Sackville-West and her husband, Harold Nicholson, bought in 1930 and where they restored the gardens in the Elizabethan style. However, whilst these two places are indeed fascinating, there are other, less famous gardens that are sure to enchant visitors such as Scotney Castle, Groombridge Place and Owl House.

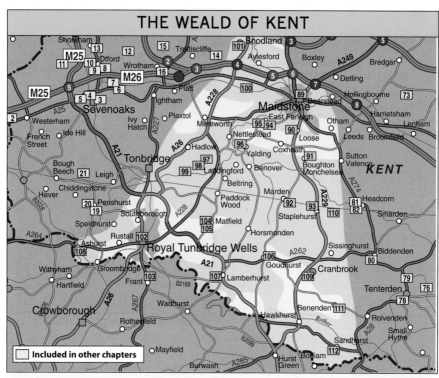

THE WEALD OF KENT

© MAPS IN MINUTES ™ (2000)

Included in other chapters

PLACES TO STAY, EAT, DRINK AND SHOP

MAIDSTONE

Maidstone grew up on the site of an important meeting place and this is reflected in the town's name that means 'the people's stone'. Meanwhile, the River Medway, on which it stands, is the ancient boundary that separated East and West Kent with the Kentish men living in the west and, to the east of the river, the men of Kent. This important distinction is still used proudly by many of the county's inhabitants today. Despite being extensively developed in the 20th century, Maidstone has retained many handsome Elizabethan and Georgian buildings and, in particular, there is the **Chillington Manor**. A beautiful Elizabethan residence, the manor is now home to the **Maidstone Museum and Art Gallery** that was founded by generous Maidstone Victorian gentlemen and that holds one of the finest collections in the south east. Amongst the many exhibits

here, that cover a wide range of interests such as oriental art, ethnography, archaeology and social history, the museum also has The Lambeth Bible Volume Two - a particularly outstanding example of 12th century illumination - and a real Egyptian mummy. Meanwhile, the equally impressive art gallery includes works by both English and continental old masters among its permanent displays.

Another part of the museum's collection can be found at **The Tyrwhitt-Drake Museum of Carriage** where visitors can see a marvellous range of horse drawn carriages that were enthusiastically collected by Sir Garrard Tyrwhitt-Drake, a former mayor of the town, who wanted to preserve this method of transport as it was being replaced by motorcars. The first collection of its kind in Britain, the museum opened in 1946 and it is housed, appropriately enough, in some stables that once belonged to the archbishops of Canterbury. Opposite these stables is the **Archbishop's Palace** that dates from the 14th century - although there was a building here at the time of the Domesday Book - and it was used as a resting place by the archbishops as they travelled between London and Canterbury. Restored and recently refurbished, the palace still retains many of its original features and, along with seeing the historic meeting room here, visitors can also enjoy refreshment at the palace's coffee shop. Meanwhile, close by are the **Dungeons**, a 14th century building from which, it is alleged, Wat Tyler, leader of

Archbishops Palace

the Peasants' Revolt in 1381, released John Ball, the 'mad priest of Kent'.

Other interesting buildings in the town that are worth seeking out include the **College of Priests**, that was founded in 1395 and is now used by the Kent Music School, and the 13th century **Corpus Christi Fraternity Hall**, where business was carried out in medieval times.

Just north of the town centre, at **Sandling**, on the banks of the River Medway, stands **Allington Castle**, the home of Sir Thomas Wyatt, one of the 'silver poets' of the 16th century and author of *They flee from me that sometime did me seek*. He shares, with the Earl of Surrey, the credit for introducing into English poetry the sonnet form that was popularised by the Italian poet, Petrarch, and that Shakespeare later went on to perfect. It was also at this castle that Henry VIII is said to have first met Anne Boleyn and, now housed in Maidstone Museum, is a chair from the castle that is a fitting testimony to this man who loved women. The chair bears the following inscription: "... of this (chay)re iss entytled too one salute from everie ladie thott settes downe in itt - Castell Alynton 1530 - Hen. 8 Rex."

Lying on the opposite bank of the Medway from the castle is **Tyland Barn** a beautifully restored 17th century building that houses the **Museum of Kent Life**. Reflecting the unique character of this area of Britain and set in some 50 acres of land at the foot of the North Downs, the museum covers many aspects of the county from some of its historic buildings, hops and a working farm to riverside and country walks.

THE SOURCE CAFE BAR

4-6 Rose Yard, Maidstone, Kent ME14 1HN
Tel: 01622 677277

The Source Cafe Bar is located in the heart of Maidstone, just off the High Street, and is housed within the former fire station. The Source has a dual personality, opening as a fashionable restaurant and bar during the day becoming a trendy music bar at night. The decor is modern and streamlined using light wood combined with brushed steel and glass in elegant curves, with concealed lighting adding unexpected highlights.

Throughout the day visitors can enjoy food from a fine and varied menu offering a selection of light dishes and snacks with cuisine from across the world being represented. The meals are freshly prepared to order and elegantly presented with everyone being assured of finding something to suit their taste and appetite. There is a fine wine list and a good selection of champagne, together with a choice of lager, soft and hot drinks.

At night this becomes a popular bar with music from a DJ each Thursday, Friday and Saturday. Open until late (until 1 am Thursday to Saturday) to over 21's only, there is a small admission charge payable after 10.30pm. If the closing time is too early, the owners also run the nearby Loft Bar which is open until 4pm on Fridays and Saturdays.

SOUTH AND WEST OF MAIDSTONE

OTHAM
3 miles SE of Maidstone off the A274

Despite being only a short distance from Maidstone, this elevated village is a haven of tranquillity with its restored 14th century church, solid yeomen's houses and surrounding orchards. Whilst, William Stevens, the writer who called himself 'Nobody' and founded the society of 'Nobody's Friends' lies buried in the churchyard it is **Stoneacre**, a National Trust property, that draws people to the village. A small and charming 15th century half-timbered yeoman's house, complete with a great hall, the delightful gardens here have been restored to their original cottage style.

LEEDS
4½ miles SE of Maidstone on the B2163

Whilst most people come to the village on their way to see the 'most beautiful castle in the World', it would be a mistake not to spend some time looking around

Thorpe Hall Drawing Room

Leeds itself. The village stands on the grounds of a former abbey, that flourished up until it was dissolved in the 16th century, and many of the older buildings in Leeds, such as its oast houses, Norman Church of St Nicholas, and surrounding farms, were part of the abbey complex.

Covering almost 1,200 years of history, **Leeds Castle** stands on two islands in the middle of the River Len and, while the peaceful moat is the home of swans and ducks, the castle itself is surrounded by beautifully landscaped **Gardens**. Built on the site of a manor house that was owned by Saxon kings, the present castle was built just after the Norman Conquest and, when Edward I came to the throne, it became a royal palace. Beloved by Henry VIII, Leeds Castle

Leeds Castle

VALE HOUSE

Old Loose Hill, Loose, near Maidstone, Kent ME15 0BH
Tel: 01622 743339 Fax: 01622 743103
e-mail: vansegethin@hotmail.com website: vanse.co.uk

Found opposite the village inn **Vale House** is a friendly and charming bed and breakfast establishment owned and run by Vanse and Tony Gethin. The house, that is surrounded by a large and colourful garden, dates from 1720 and it stands on the site of a tannery which typifies the local industry of the time that also included fulling, dyeing and paper mills.

Very much a family home, Vanse and Tony have lived here since 1970, each of the three guest bedrooms are beautifully furnished and decorated, as is the rest of the house, and everything is provided to ensure that guests have a peaceful night's sleep, including an abundance of books. With a real home from home atmosphere, where nothing is too much trouble, guests take breakfast seated around a large refectory table in the dining room that overlooks the magnificent garden. The ideal place for a relaxing stay, Vale House is a place that is well worth seeking out.

WIERTON HALL FARM

East Hall Hill,
Boughton Monchelsea,
near Maidstone,
Kent ME17 4JU
Tel: 01622 743535
Fax: 01622 743535

Surrounded by working arable farmland, **Wierton Hall Farm** has an attractive 300 year old farmhouse that is built of the local ragstone with typical Kent peg tiles. From their delightful home, Jackie and Robin Robertson offer friendly and relaxed bed and breakfast accommodation in a choice of three comfortable guest bedrooms. Anyone staying here will immediately feel

at home due to the friendly nature and careful attention to detail of their hosts. A cosy guest lounge, with a wood burning stove that is lit on colder evenings, is the place to relax and read or chat to fellow guests. Jackie is a wonderful cook and the excellent breakfasts, that can be tailored to guest's special requirements, are served in the elegant dining room. An evening meal can also be served by prior arrangement. There are several good walks straight from the farm and the family have plenty of local knowledge that they are happy to pass on to visitors.

Leeds Castle

BROOMFIELD
5 miles SE of Maidstone off the A20

This picturesque village in the Len Valley was mentioned in the Domesday Book and, in the churchyard of its 12th century church, lie buried several members of both the Wykeham-Martins and Fairfax families of Leeds Castle along with Frederick Hollands, a 19th century county cricketer from Broomfield. It is also the home of a 1,000 year old yew tree.

LOOSE
2½ miles S of Maidstone off the A229

was relinquished by the crown in the mid 16th century and, from then onwards, it has been in private hands. The last owner, an American heiress, Olive, Lady Baillie, bought the estate in 1926 and it is thanks to her vision, determination and hard work that Leeds Castle is so impressive today. One of the most popular visitor attractions in the country, there is plenty to delight and interest the public both inside and in the gardens. Not only is the castle home to the **Dog Collar Museum**, the finest such collection in the world, but many of the gardens have been restored including the maze and grotto and the informal and typically English Culpepper Garden. One new garden is particularly interesting - the Lady Baillie Garden - and it honours the woman who put so much back into the castle before her death in 1974. Here are planted numerous sub tropical species like bananas and tree palms that flourish in this south facing site.

Pronounced 'Looze', the older part of this delightful village lies in a narrow little valley and the cottages rise in terraces above the stream. The power of the stream, along with its purity and the availability of Fullers Earth, helped to established a flourishing woollen industry here in the 16th century but, as the trade decline, some of the mills were converted to paper making. This change of direction brought about more contact with Maidstone, just to the north, and the village is slowly being absorbed by its larger neighbour. The viaduct that carries the main road from Maidstone across the Loose valley was built by Thomas Telford in 1829 and, along this stretch of road, can be seen large stones that were used, with the help of ropes, to pull heavy wagons up the hill.

BOUGHTON MONCHELSEA
3½ miles S of Maidstone on the B2163

Found on a ridge overlooking the Weald of Kent, this pleasant village was at the centre of Kentish ragstone quarrying and,

THE UNICORN

High Street, Marden, Kent TN12 9DR
Tel: 01622 831426
e-mail: kcrookledge@supanet.com

Found in the heart of Marden, The Unicorn is an attractive old inn that dates from the early 17th century and that has, tucked away to the rear, a secluded, landscaped beer garden complete with patio area where barbecues are held in the summer.

This is very much a traditional inn, there are no fruit machines or loud music although one area of the open plan bar has been put aside for games such as Monopoly and Trivial Pursuits. In this olde worlde atmosphere, customers to the inn can also enjoy the warmth generated by the roaring log fire in the large inglenook fireplace and take a look at some of the daily newspaper and magazines that landlords, Keith and Rosalynd Rookledge put out for customers.

A friendly and welcoming inn that is highly regarded for its well stocked bar, The Unicorn has a fine reputation for the high standard of the food served here. The traditional menu includes many favourites but undoubtedly the house speciality here are the home-made pies and, as well as the more usual beer and ale pies, there are such imaginative and mouthwatering choices as duck and damson and rosemary and chicken. The Sunday roast lunches too are popular and, when in season, game features on the menu. A delightful, friendly inn, where several local groups meet throughout the week, this is an inviting place that welcomes children as well as adults.

THE COACH HOUSE

Thorford Hall Farm, Staplehurst, Kent TN12 0HQ
Tel: 01580 891353 Fax: 01580 891353
e-mail: rlusty@virgin.net
website: www.thorfordhall.co.uk

Situated just a few minutes from the village of Staplehurst, **The Coach House** is an attractive farm conversion that lies close to Thorford Hall Farm's 17th century farmhouse. The conversion work on The Coach House has been done to a very high standard and, as well as providing charming cottage style accommodation, the interior is immaculate. All the furnishings and decorations are of the highest quality and, briefly, this comfortable and cosy cottage comprises a pleasant lounge, a fully equipped kitchen and a charming double bedroom with en suite bathroom. The addition of a sofa bed in the lounge provides accommodation here for four although The Coach House is not suitable for children under 12 or family pets. The Coach House operates a non smoking policy.

However, whilst this cottage is indeed charming it is the little extras that owner, Diane Lusty,

provides that makes all the difference here. A welcome pack, with all that is needed for breakfast, is left for new guests and the patio area outside the cottage has a table and chairs so that the very best can be made of this superb location. Surrounded by gardens and the farmland, guests can see the paddocks with the award winning Lusty herd of Dexter cattle. Diane is happy to show guests around the farm and to tell them more about this small breed.

not surprisingly, this local building material features heavily here. The quarries, on the edge of the village, have been worked almost continuously for seven centuries but archaeologists suggest that they were used longer ago than that as both the Romans and the Saxon used the stone in their buildings. Some of these stones were used in the construction of Westminster Abbey and Henry III ordered a number of cannonballs to be made from Kentish ragstone. Naturally, the village's 13th century parish Church of St Peter was built with this readily available material. It is also home to one of the oldest lychgates in England - erected in 1470 the gate was built entirely without nails.

To the north of the church lies **Boughton Monchelsea Place**, a beautiful fortified ragstone manor house, that was originally built in 1567, that provides breathtaking views of the surrounding private deer park and unspoilt countryside. Inside, the house visitors can see a wealth of antique furniture, pictures and tapestries along with the galleried Jacobean staircase whilst, outside, there is a delightful walled garden and courtyard. Here, too, can be seen a collection of carriages and early farming implements.

MARDEN
7 miles S of Maidstone on the B2079

Surrounded by orchards and hop fields, the old part of the village is centred around the main street that is lined with attractive tile hung and weatherboarded houses. This village was, centuries ago, part of a Royal Hundred and, as it was exempt from the jurisdiction of the County Sheriff, it had its own court. This ancient court house still stands in the old square but the village stocks have been moved and can now be found in the porch of Marden's 13th century church.

STAPLEHURST
8 miles S of Maidstone on the A229

There was once a stronghold in the village but, today, all that can be seen is a tree covered mound and little is known of the fortification's history. In 1865, the novelist Charles Dickens was involved in a serious train accident at the point where the track crosses the River Beult, that lies to the east of Staplehurst, and he makes a reference to this in a postscript to his novel *Our Mutual Friend*.

A garden with a difference, **Iden Court Herbs** has wonderful displays of herbs, aromatic wild flowers and plants that particularly attract butterflies, in both open and walled gardens. It is also home to the national oreganum and mentha collections and, along with the special events held here, there is a café for refreshments. Another place in the village that is well worth a visit, is the charming and interesting museum - **Brattle Farm Museum** - where a wide ranging collection of vintage cars, tractors, veterinary equipment, horses and harnesses, weights and measures and Victorian and Edwardian household items are displayed along with other exhibits that relate to rural life.

EAST FARLEIGH
2 miles SW of Maidstone on the B2010

Standing on steeply rising ground on the side of the River Medway, East Farleigh is surrounded by orchards and overlooks a graceful 14th century bridge. It was over this superb five-arched river crossing that Parliamentary soldiers marched, in 1648, on their way to capture Maidstone from the Royalists during the Civil War. One of the most important engagements in the war, the battle left 300 of the King's supporters dead and more than 1,000 were taken prisoner. In the churchyard of the village's ancient church, a cross marks the final resting place of 43 hop pickers who died of cholera whilst working here in 1849. Also in the churchyard can be found the graves of the artist Donald Maxwell and the wife of the reformer William Wilberforce.

NETTLESTEAD
5 miles SW of Maidstone on the B2015

A quiet village set on a bank above a particularly pleasant stretch of the River Medway, Nettlestead is home to two buildings that are thought to have been founded by Bishop Odo, the half-brother of William the Conqueror. The present parish **Church of St Mary** was rebuilt in 1420 and it contains some lovely stained glass windows that were greatly damaged in 1763 when a thunderstorm unleashed 10 inch hailstones on the village. Beside the church stands **Nettlestead Place**, an ancient private house that contains a medieval undercroft.

THE FARLEIGH BULL

Lower Road, East Farleigh,
near Maidstone, Kent ME15 0HD
Tel: 01622 726282
Fax: 01622 725809
e-mail: Russell@Farleigh-Bull.co.uk
website: www.Farleigh-Bull.co.uk

Found in the heart of this delightful village, **The Farleigh Bull** is a spacious and popular place that dates from 1910 when it replaced the former pub that had been destroyed by fire. Just across the road is a reminder that the original Farleigh Bull was a coaching inn in the form of a time worn mounting block that stands beneath a huge chestnut tree. Also close by is the village church, a useful landmark, whilst to the rear of this inn is a large beer garden that provides glorious views over the local countryside from this elevated position. Despite the building's age, the interior of the inn is very olde worlde and it transports customers back to the days of stagecoach travel - there are dark ceiling beams, converted gaslights and oil lamps, shelves of books and some interesting pictures of bygone days in East Farleigh hanging from the wood panelled walls.

Very much at the hub of village life and a popular meeting place, landlords Susan and Russell Roberts ensure that there is always a

good selection of real ales on tap, as well as all the usual beers, lagers and spirits, to quench their customers' thirst. The food here, too, is excellent and the menu offers customers an extensive range of quality dishes that are all reasonably priced whilst their traditional Sunday roast lunches are also very popular and it is necessary to book here to avoid disappointment. The regular live music held here covers a variety of tastes and children, in particular, will be delighted with their play area and the small zoo out in the garden where they can meet Winston, the pot-bellied pig, and other animals.

THE VICTORY

Farleigh Bridge, East
Farleigh,
near Maidstone,
Kent ME16 9NB
Tel: 01622 726591

Benefiting from a lovely position - high up on an elevated site overlooking the river - **The Victory** is a popular pub that attracts a good number of sailors and walkers in addition to having a loyal local following.

A large beer garden makes the best use of both the available space and the location, as it looks back down on the river. A hundred people can be seated here comfortably and, in the summer, there are barbecues and special play areas for children.

The inside of this free house is no disappointment either: there are three separate areas each with its own snack bar. Brickfaced fireplaces offer a cheery warmth in two of the bars and the snug bar features some original bar billiards. Publican Mike Kidner has been in the trade for 35 years and presides over a selection of three lagers, four bitters and four real ales. The food served here is also excellent and has earned The Victory an enviable local reputation, with the home-cooked choices ranging from bar snacks to a full à la carte menu in the new restaurant section.

YALDING
5 miles SW of Maidstone on the B2010

This lovely village's position, at the confluence of the Rivers Medway, Beult and Teise, provides ample irrigation for the fertile soil so it is not surprising that Yalding lies in one of the largest hop-growing parishes in England. Each of the three rivers here are crossed by their own medieval bridge whilst the delightful high street is lined with charming weatherboarded houses that date back to the 17th century. At **Yalding Organic Gardens** visitors can see 14 individual gardens, including a Tudor garden, a Victorian garden and a wildlife garden, that illustrate the history of gardening from medieval times through to the present day. Changing ideas and themes down the ages are also highlighted such as

stewardship of resource, the importance of genetic engineering and organic horticulture.

LADDINGFORD
6½ miles SW of Maidstone off the A228

This ancient village, that is really little more than a hamlet, grew up around a

Cottage and Old English Garden, Benover

THE WALNUT TREE

Yalding Hill, Yalding, Kent ME18 6JB
Tel: 01622 814266

Built in 1472 as a Tudor yeoman's house, **The Walnut Tree** was then described as a four bay dwelling as it had four bays - or rooms - although one of the rooms is, in this case, a massive fireplace although it was once the house's kitchen. As might be imagined by the age of the building, there of low beamed ceilings and, in order to go from one of the rooms to another, customers step up (or down) rather than go through doorways. Throughout, in the bar and restaurant areas, hop bines hang from the walls and ceilings

that provide a reminder to the days then the village was inundated with Londoners taking a holiday in the countryside whilst also bringing in the hop harvest.

A charming and interesting old building, it is however, the excellent selection of real ales, beers, lagers and the wonderful food that draw people to The Walnut Tree. Chef, David Telfer, prepares a superb à la carte menu and, whether dining in style in the restaurant, or taking a bar snack, customers can be assured that everything is home-made, on the premises, and is not only well presented but also absolutely delicious. Booking, particularly at weekends, is essential.

THE ROSE AND CROWN

Branbridges Road, East Peckham, Kent TM12 5HD
Tel: 01622 871202

Just ten minutes drive from The Walnut Tree and owned by the same proprietor, Barry Jenner, **The Rose and Crown**, whilst not having the historic connections of The Walnut Tree does live up to its same high standards of hospitality. A victim of the severe flooding that affected this area in December 2000 (it lies just 100 feet from the River Medway), The Rose and Crown has been completely refurbished and the large open plan bar area gives the inn a feeling of space although, those wanting a more intimate setting, will find that there is a separate snug.

Again, food is a key feature of The Rose and Crown and there is a speciality carvery, from Tuesday to Sunday afternoons, that can be found in the separate restaurant. In the evenings the menu changes and, over seen by David Telfer from the Walnut Tree, this à la carte menu is, once again, an excellent tribute to the very best in traditional English cuisine.

ford on a tributary of the River Medway. In nearly every direction there are orchards but, looking south from the village, there is a wooded ridge with Goudhurst at its crest.

BELTRING
7½ miles SW of Maidstone on the A228

This neat little village is home to one of the county's major attractions - the **Whitbread Hop Farm**. Situated on a 1,000 acre working hop farm, this agricultural complex was originally a hop-drying centre supplying this major brewery but it has grown to house a museum, a rural crafts centre and a natural trail. As well as learning about the history and purpose of hops in the brewing process - until the 14th century cloves were more commonly used as flavouring - and also the brewing industry itself, visitors, and particularly children, will enjoy meeting the famous Whitbread

shire horses and the smaller animals at the pets corner. A collection of agricultural machinery is on display and, along with the exhibition of rural crafts, there is a choice of restaurants.

HADLOW
9 miles SW of Maidstone on the A26

Lying in the Medway Valley, this attractive village has a wide main street where a number of its older houses can be found. These, and the rest of the village, are, however, completely overshadowed by the curiosity known as **May's Folly**. A tower some 170 feet high, this is all that remains of Hadlow Castle that was built by the eccentric industrialist Walter Barton May over a number of years and was finally finished in the early 19th century. A landmark for miles around, May built the tower so that he would have a view that extended as far as the south coast but, unfortunately, the South

THE MAN OF KENT,

226 Tonbridge Road, Little Mill, East Peckham, Kent TN12 5LA Tel: 01622 871345

The Man of Kent is a delightful traditional coaching inn dating back to 1588. It has many attractive features, including the low beamed ceilings, oak doors and large inglenook fireplace. Old beer tankards and amusing brass plaques adorn the beams. Licensees Ben Ryan and Kelly Stoney took over on 29th February 2000; originally from Manchester, their goal is to provide top-quality food and drink which can be enjoyed in the friendliest possible surroundings - a goal they are well on their way to achieving, as befits their personal motto: Good Beer, Good Food, Good Company. A mix of locals and visitors rub shoulders quite happily, comprising walkers, tourists, boaters off the Medway and more.

The pub is just two minutes' walk from the Medway's banks, in a peaceful location on the edge of East Peckham. Lying close to a hop farm, it is surrounded by orchards and oast houses. The area is crisscrossed with public footpaths, including the famous Medway Walk. To one side of the inn, the River Bourne runs within six feet of the large and attractive beer garden. People come from miles around to feed the huge Chubb that make this river their home. Harveys and Larkins are the resident ales, and there are always two additional guest ales. There's an impressive selection of wines, as well as a good complement of spirits and soft drinks. The food is also worth a special trip, as it is all home cooked and home prepared, and features selections from five large specials boards including seafood dishes, superb salads, delicious Sunday roasts and many other tempting options. The menu changes with the seasons, to ensure that the freshest ingredients are always made use of.

THE BELL INN

Three Elm Lane, Golden Green,
Tonbridge, Kent TN11 0BD
Tel: 01732 851748

The attractive **Bell Inn** in Golden Green is a traditional English pub at its most welcoming. Owners Justine and Andy are friendly and convivial hosts enjoying their first venture in the pub trade. This charming pub is a popular spot for locals, ramblers, cyclists and boat enthusiasts. A vintage motorcycle rally is held nearby. A play area for children is underway and the peaceful setting here in the middle of this quiet village on the River Medway – just a 10 minute walk from Hadlow Castle in the heart of the hop and fruit-growing region – enhances guests' enjoyment of the fine food and drink on offer.

Built in the 16th century with 17th and 18th century additions, one of the outside walls is carved with the initials of the villagers who left to fight the Boer War. The interior has beamed ceilings, real fires and a wealth of photographs spanning over 100 years of local history. Outside there's a courtyard patio with seating.

Food is available in the bar or in the separate welcoming dining area. The menu changes according to what's available at its most fresh, and all dishes are home-made. A sample of the hearty traditional meals on offer includes game pie, grilled sardines, cheese and asparagus flan and venison casserole. Tasty bar snacks are also available. To wash down the excellent food, there's Triumph, Abbot and IPA ales, a changing guest ale, and a good selection of soft drinks, wines and spirits. Occasional theme nights are well worth making a special visit for.

BLACKLANDS HOUSE

Blacklands, East Malling,
near Maidstone, Kent ME19 6DS
Tel: 01732 844274
e-mail: blacklands@tinyonline.co.uk

Anyone looking for a pampered overnight stay in lovely surroundings should look no further than **Blacklands House**, an elegant Georgian residence in a quiet hamlet that is only four miles from Maidstone. Built in 1830 for a local mill owner and gentleman farmer, the house stands in attractive gardens with a stream, lake and waterfall nearby.

Blacklands House retains many of its original features and the floor-to-ceiling French windows on the ground floor make the interior light and airy. Chandeliers and other furnishings reflect the origins of the house, which has its original shutters still in place and in the dining room, which overlooks the garden, there is an imposing archway. Meanwhile, the guests' drawing room, which too overlooks the garden though on two sides, is a comfortable and inviting place where daily papers, books and a television are available for guests. The five guest rooms are spacious and full of character. Owner Ann Leonard takes great pride in both the house and the high standard of hospitality that she offers. A full English breakfast is served to guests in the dining room and the dietary requirements of guests can easily be accommodated. Not surprisingly, many people return to this quiet and secluded house.

Downs made this particular dream of his impossible.

Anyone looking for gardening ideas in the heart of the Garden of England should pay a visit to **Broadview Gardens** where the belief of the success of a garden lying in its design is firmly held. There are a wide range of gardens to see here - from subtropical, stone and water, oriental and Italian to mixed borders, cottage, bog and wildlife. Beside the more traditional gardens there are experimental areas and this is an ideal place to come to for anyone looking for gardening inspiration. Though wandering around Broadview is extremely interesting it can also be thirsty work and there is a friendly restaurant at the gardens.

AYLESFORD
13 miles NE of Sevenoaks off the A20

This picturesque village is not only one of Kent's oldest villages but it has, over the centuries, seen more than its fair share of fighting. Having travelled many miles from Pegwell Bay, the Jutish leaders Hengist and Horsa defeated the ancient Britons here in a great battle in AD 455. Though Horsa died in the battle, Hengist along with his son Aesc established a kingdom here (Cantware - or 'men of Kent') and, for the next 300 years, the land was ruled by the descendants of Aesc, the dynasty of the Eskings. Later, in 893, the Danes were seen off by King Alfred whilst, soon afterwards, in 918, Edmund Ironside defeated Canute and the Vikings at Aylesford.

Thankfully, times became a little more peaceful and, in 1242, when the first Carmelites arrived here from the Holy Land, they founded **Aylesford Priory**. After the Dissolution in the 16th century, the priory became a private house and was rebuilt in 1675 only to be destroyed by a fire in the 1930s. After World War II, in 1949, the Carmelites took over the house and, having restored it to its former

THE FREEMASONS ARMS

Brook Lane, Ham Hill,
Snodland,
Kent ME6 5OR
Tel: 01634 240211

Since landlords, Janet and Tony Capon first came to **The Freemasons Arms**, in 1992, they have seen this local inn become a popular and busy place and, certainly, the hospitality on offer here is friendly and professional.

Divided into a bar and a restaurant area inside, this large, open plan pub has plenty of space for its customers and the atmosphere here is surprisingly cosy - due no doubt to the open fire, wood panelled walls and the displays of dried flowers. Along with the large customer car park, there is also a terraced garden, ideal in the summer, that has various children's play things including a wooden climbing frame.

A wide range of drinks are available from the bar including a local real ale from Chatham and there is a good choice of wine. With Tony busy at the bar, Janet attends to the food and she ensures that all the dishes served here are home-made. From bar snacks through to a full à la carte menu there is sure to be something for everyone and children have their own special menu.

THORIN'S WINE BAR AND RESTAURANT

9 Nevill Street, Tunbridge Wells, Kent TN2 5RU
Tel: 01892 531480 Fax: 01892 548115

Thorin's Wine Bar and Restaurant enjoys a prime location in the centre of Tunbridge Wells, situated on the corner of Nevill Street and Warwick Park. The stylish building is a well preserved example of some of the fine architecture to be found in the town. It has been well preserved and is attractively presented with the addition of colourful flowering baskets.

The wine bar and restaurant are located upstairs and are of an equally high standard with a wooden floor extending throughout matching the wooden banisters, beams and large bar. To one side there are a number of small tables and high stools at which to enjoy a drink while the adjoining dining area is simply furnished with the wooden dining tables being dressed with clean white table

cloths and fresh flowers. The emphasis here is clearly on the very high standard of freshly prepared dishes that are served. The a la carte menu offers an excellent choice of meat, fish and vegetarian dishes with some lighter snacks also available. Daily specials can offer some even more delightful choices such as Baked Lemon Sole, Paella and Black Tiger Shrimp skewers.

In addition to a wide selection of red and white wines from around the world, the bar also stocks a number of real ales and draught lager. The bar and restaurant are open every day at lunch time and in the evening. Advance bookings are recommended at weekends to avoid disappointment.

THE GEORGE INN

36 High Street, Frant,
East Sussex TN3 9DU
Tel: 01892 750350
Fax: 01892 750921
www: the georgefrant@aol.com

Found in the heart of this village, which lies just over the county border in East Sussex, **The George Inn** is a delightful, traditional country inn that stands opposite the village school and beside the church. A striking black and white building that originally dates from the 1600s, a plaque close to the entrance of the inn was presented to the people of Frant by the Canadian government in memory of Lieutenant Colonel John Byre, the founder of Bytown (later renamed Ottawa). Byre died in 1836 and lies buried in the village churchyard. The owners of The George Inn, Pat and Peter Rogers, continue the connections Frant has with north America as Pat is originally from California. Now both settled at the inn since moving here in October 2000, this hospitable couple offer a warm welcome and a friendly environment to all who enter The George. A good range of real ales and wines are available from the bar where the low ceilings and large inglenook fireplace add to the already cosy atmosphere. There is a separate dining room, again with a very traditional feel, that overlooks the garden and here customers can enjoy a wide range of homecooked dishes from the delicious menu. Old favourites are a speciality here and, along with the traditional pub food, the roast rib of beef and the extensive vegetarian selections also prove to be popular. A charming country inn with a real village feel, The George Inn is well worth taking the trouble to visit.

glory, they have re-established the priory - now calling its **The Friars** to use its traditional name. Today, it is a peaceful and tranquil retreat set in acres of well tended grounds in which visitors are invited to picnic. The restored 17th century barn acts as a tea rooms, as well as a gift and bookshop, whilst the chapels contain some outstanding modern works of religious art. Still a popular place for pilgrimage, there is also a guesthouse here that offers peace and quiet to individuals, groups and families and there are extensive conference facilities.

Whilst the priory is certainly one of the village's places of interest, the charm of Aylesford, situated on the banks of the River Medway, cannot easily be ignored. This has been an important river crossing for centuries and records recall that there was a bridge spanning the river here as long ago as 1287. However, the beautiful five-arched **Bridge** seen today dates from the 14th century and from it there is an excellent view of Aylesford's delightful half-timbered, steeply gabled cottages.

Just north of the village lies further evidence of the long history of settlement in and around Aylesford in the form of **Kits Coty House**. Situated on Blue Bell Hill, this is a Neolithic burial chamber (with a capstone lying across three huge upright stones) that is reputed to be the tomb of a British chieftain who was killed by the Jutish leader Horsa. Whether this is true or just local legend matters little as the views from the monument, out across the valley to the Medway Gap, make a walk to this site very worth while.

ROYAL TUNBRIDGE WELLS

Surrounded by the unspoilt beauty of the Weald, some of the most scenic areas of countryside in England, Royal Tunbridge

Wells is a pretty and attractive town that has been a popular place to visit for several hundred years. However, unlike many of the major towns and cities of Kent, Royal Tunbridge Wells has no Roman or ecclesiastical heritage and, during the Middle Ages, when many towns were establishing their trading reputations, it was little more than a forest. The secret of how this charming place gained such prominence lies in the 'Royal' and 'Wells' of its name. In 1606, the courtier, Dudley, Lord North, found chalybeate springs here and he rushed back to court to break the news of his discovery of what he declared to be health giving waters. Soon the fashionable from London were taking the water and spreading the word of their health restoring qualities but, for three decades, there were no buildings beside the springs.

In 1630, Tunbridge Wells received its first royal visitor when Queen Henrietta Maria, the wife of Charles I, came here to recuperate after giving birth to the future Charles II. She and her entourage, like other visitors, camped on the grounds by the springs. However, soon afterwards, enterprising local people began to build here but the real development of the town into one of the most popular spas of the 18th and 19th centuries was due to the Earl of Abergavenny. In order to increase the popularity of the spa, Beau Nash, the famous dandy who played an important role in the development of another spa town, Bath, came here as Master of Ceremonies in 1735. With Nash at the helm, guiding and even dictating fashion, Tunbridge Wells went from strength to strength and, whilst royalty had always found the town to their liking, it was granted its 'Royal' prefix in 1909 by Edward VII.

The chalybeate spring that was

The Wells Exhibit

accidentally discovered by Lord North whilst out riding in what was then Waterdown Forest still flows in front of the **Bath House**, that was built in 1804 on top of the original Cold Bath. Meanwhile, close to the original springs was a grassy promenade known as The Walks where those coming to take the waters could take some exercise. In 1699 Princess Anne visited Tunbridge Wells with her son, the Duke of Gloucester, who slipped and hurt himself along The Walks. The irate Princess complained and the town authorities tiled over the grass and so created **The Pantiles** that remains, today, a lovely shaded walk that is lined with elegant shops. The Pantiles were the central focal point for the hectic social life

arranged by Beau Nash and there were concerts and balls throughout the season along with gambling houses. Also found in this area of the town is the **Church of King Charles the Martyr** that is often dubbed the 'jewel of the Pantiles'. Originally established as a chapel in 1678 for those coming to take the waters, the church has been extended and one of its most interesting features is the charming clock that was donated to the church in 1760 by Lavinia Fenton, the actress and mistress of the Duke of Bolton. Meanwhile, inside, there is a superb ceiling that was created by Henry Doogood, the chief plasterer to Sir Christopher Wren.

For a greater insight into the history and development of the town, a visit to the **Royal Tunbridge Wells Museum and Art Galley** that was opened in 1952 is a must. Amongst the displays and exhibits on natural history and art, there is an exhibition of local history and a collection of Tunbridge ware - the decorative woodwork that is unique to the area.

Once part of the extensive network of railway lines in Kent and neighbouring

THE STAR INN

Maidstone Road, Matfield, Kent TN12 7JR
Tel: 01892 722041

A short drive heading north east of Tunbridge Wells brings travellers to the small village of Matfield. Here you will find the Star Inn which presents an attractive frontage to the main road. Run by Sue and John Clarke for the past eleven years, the charming building dates back in parts to the 15th century and features a spacious, yet cosy, interior that is attractively decorated and furnished. Open all day, every day, the bar offers three real ales, a regularly changing guest ale, together with the usual selection of beer and lager. Food is available each lunch time and evening and there is a separate dining area seating 50 diners. There are three guest rooms available for overnight bed and breakfast accommodation.

East Sussex, **Spa Valley Railway** is a restored and preserved section of this system that was re-opened in 1996. Now running between Royal Tunbridge Wells and High Rocks, the trains leave Tunbridge Wells West station and take passengers on a pleasant journey through the Wealden countryside.

AROUND ROYAL TUNBRIDGE WELLS

MATFIELD
5 miles NE of Royal Tunbridge Wells on the B2160

At the centre of this village is one of the largest village greens in Kent and around it old and new houses blend harmoniously including several fine tile hung, typically Kentish houses and an impressive Georgian dwelling.

THE WHEELWRIGHTS ARMS

The Green, Matfield, Tonbridge, Kent TN12 7JX
Tel/Fax: 01892 722129

With a picturesque location at the corner of the village green, **The Wheelwrights Arms** makes an ideal spot to linger over a drink outside while a cricket match unfolds opposite on a long summer afternoon. This handsome white weatherboard pub was built in 1602 and was originally three cottages forming part of a larger estate. Through the centuries its role has changed, first as a grocery and bakery, then adding beer to the goods on offer in the mid-18th century. It assumed its present appearance around 1750, when it was first licensed as an ale house. The extensive beer garden boasts a covered area, beneath a charming canopy. On winter days, customers are met by a roaring log fire within the huge inglenook fireplace.

Chrissie and Arthur Powell, the proprietors, run this family-run establishment with help from their daughter Emma, who assists in the bar and restaurant. Chrissie plans to open a bric-a-brac shop on the premises soon, to showcase and sell local crafts. Arthur enjoys sharing his knowledge about the pub and its history, while Christine provides the home-baked gammon and other hearty fare that have customers coming back again and again. The menu includes a fine range of hearty and delicious dishes, such as steak and ale pie, breast of duck, shell of prawns, steaks and more - all home cooked. Cream teas are also available in summer. An interesting mix of patrons includes local villagers, players from the local cricket and polo teams, cyclists, walkers and pilots from the local airport. Upstairs are two charming guest bedrooms which are available for B&B. Scotney Castle, Marle Place and a local hop farm are all within easy distance, as are many other interesting and picturesque places to enjoy a day out.

HORSMONDEN
7½ miles E of Tunbridge Wells on the B2162

Pronounced 'Horzm'den', it is hard to imagine that this delightful village, tucked amongst orchards and fields, was once a thriving industrial centre. Although little evidence of this remains today the key to the village's prosperity lies in the pond found just to the west of Horsmonden. Known as a furnace pond, it supplied water to the ironworks that flourished in the

Vegetable Garden, Horsmonden

Weald of Kent. Now, nature is reclaiming the pond and it will soon be indistinguishable from other expanses of water found in and around the village.

From the village green, that is known as The Heath, a footpath leads to the village church that lies some two miles to the west. This is a walk worth making as the countryside is pleasant and, on reaching the church, visitors can see a memorial to John Read, who died in 1847, and is best known for inventing the stomach pump.

GOUDHURST
9 miles E of Tunbridge Wells on the A262

Standing on a hill and with sweeping views across the surrounding orchards and hop fields, and especially over the Weald, Goudhurst (that is pronounced 'Gowdhurst') is a picturesque place that draws many visitors, not least because of its main street that is lined with traditional tile hung, weatherboarded cottages. The solidity of the village

THE VINE HOTEL

High Street, Goudhurst, Kent TN17 1AG
Tel: 01580 211261

Fifty metres from Goudhurst's lovely duck pond and village green, **The Vine Hotel** is a traditional hotel, pub and restaurant offering comfort and quality. With ample outdoor seating and tables overlooking the duck pond and in the beer garden to the rear, this fine hotel dates back in parts to the early 17th century, though is mostly 18th century in design. Brick fireplaces, wooden floors and dark oak beamwork add to the cosy ambience.

There are six handsome and very comfortable guest bedrooms, one with a superb four-poster bed. Guests' every comfort and convenience are always the standard which manager Jason McGahan and their capable and friendly staff keep in mind. The hotel's huge dining area occupies a new traditional-style conservatory. Facilities for those with disabilities are excellent. In the bar, there is a range of great beers, including guest beers and Harvey's Best Bitter, Courage Best, Larkins, London Pride and Thai, Chinese and Indian bottled beers. The wine list is extensive and very impressive.

The lunchtime menu offers a range of English favourites, including the traditional Sunday roast. At night, the three Thai chefs - the head chef has over 15 years' experience - come into their own, preparing and cooking a fantastic selection of fresh delicacies from the Thai Sawan menu. The chefs are also happy to prepare to order dishes not on the menu - but with dishes such as hot green chicken curry with coconut, stir-fried vegetables, sweet and sour pork and king prawns with garlic and ginger, there is surely something to suit every palate. The choice of appetisers and specialities is particularly impressive.

THE ELEPHANT'S HEAD

Furnace Lane, Hook Green, Lamberhurst, Kent TN3 8LT
Tel: 01892 890279

Lying almost on the Kent-Sussex border is the village of Hook Green and **The Elephant's Head**. The attractive building is clearly centuries old and features a half timbered construction with a small beer garden and children's play area to the front. The Elephant's Head has a far reaching reputation for offering a warm and friendly welcome to all who pass through the door, serving a good selection of real ales mostly from local breweries. A tasty selection of food is offered each lunch time and evening (except Sunday evening) with a regular menu and blackboard specials. Advance booking is recommended at weekends and for the very popular Sunday lunchtime carvery.

reflects the prosperity it enjoyed when the woollen industry was introduced here in the Middle Ages. The village church, which stands on the hilltop, dates chiefly from the 15th century and, inside, there are many memorials to the leading local family, the Culpeppers.

Just to the southwest of the village lies **Finchcocks** a charming Georgian manor house, with a dramatic frontage, that is named after the family who lived on this land in the 13th century. Built for the barrister, Edward Bathurst in 1725, the house has managed to retain many of its original features despite having changed hands several times over the years. In 1970, Finchcocks was bought by Richard Burnett, a leading exponent of the early piano and, today, it is home to his magnificent collection of historic keyboard instruments. The high ceilings and oak panelled rooms are the ideal setting for the beautiful instruments that include chamber organs, harpsichords, spinets and early pianos and, whenever the house is open to the public those instruments restored to concert standard are played. Along with these instruments Finchcocks also houses some fine pictures and prints and an exhibition on 18th century pleasure gardens. Meanwhile, the beautiful gardens, including the restored walled garden, provide a dramatic setting for outside events.

Further south again and adjoining the county border with East Sussex lies **Bedgebury National Pinetum and Forest Gardens**, that was founded jointly by the Forestry Commission and the Royal Botanic Gardens at Kew in the 1920s. Today, Bedgebury is home to the National Conifer Collection and within this, the finest collection of conifers in the world, are some of the most famous, including the Californian redwoods.

LAMBERHURST
6 miles SE of Royal Tunbridge Wells on the A21

As this village lies on the main road between Royal Tunbridge Wells and Hastings, it once played an important role as a coaching stop but much of the village's prosperity is due to the iron industry of the Weald. The high street here is lined with attractive old houses and other buildings dating from those days and a sample of Lamberhurst's iron railings, like the one's from the village that can be found in St Paul's Cathedral,

Oast Houses, Lamberhurst

can be seen along this road. Lamberhurst's 14th century church, too, tells of past glories and, set some way from the village centre in the valley of the River Teise, it has been remodelled to accommodate a congregation that is now smaller than those it attracted during the years of Lamberhurst's heyday. Today, the village is associated with viticulture and the first vineyard was established here in 1972.

To the northwest of the village lies **The Owl House** a particularly pretty little cottage whose tenants, according to records dating from 1522, paid the monks at Bayham Abbey an annual rental of one white cockerel. Later the house became associated with night smugglers or 'owlers' (hence its name) who traded English wool for French brandy and avoided the tax inspectors by giving out coded hoot calls. In 1952, the house was bought by Lady Dufferin and, while this is not open to the public, the beautiful **Gardens** that she planted are. There are

extensive lawns and walks through woodland of birch, beech and English oak as well as spring bulbs, roses, flowering shrubs and ornamental fruit trees. As this was once the site of the iron works that made some of the fitments for St Paul's Cathedral, there are also hammer ponds and these have been creatively converted into informal water gardens surrounded by willows, camellias and rhododendrons.

Meanwhile, to the east of the Lamberhurst lies **Scotney Castle**, a massive, rust stained tower that was built by Roger de Ashburnham in 1378 and that now incorporates the ruins of a Tudor house. However, what especially draws people to Scotney are the romantic **Gardens** that are renowned for their autumn colours but are beautiful through out the seasons. The water lily filled moat around the ruins provides the perfect centrepiece to the wealth of plants found in the gardens and there are also delightful countryside walks around the estate.

Scotney Castle

GROOMBRIDGE
4 miles SW of Royal Tunbridge Wells on the B2110

Straddling the county border between Kent and Sussex, it is generally recognised that the Kent side of this village is the prettier and more interesting as this is where the triangular village green lies, overlooked by the tile hung cottages of the Groombridge estate. This charming village centrepiece is also overlooked by **Groombridge Place**, a classical 17th century manor house that stands on the site of a medieval castle. The house is surrounded by superb parkland and **Gardens** that were designed by the famous Jacobean diarist John Evelyn in a formal manner. Likened to a series of rooms, the walled gardens are complemented by extensive herbaceous borders whilst, high above these, there is **The Enchanted Forest** a magical and imaginative series of mysterious gardens that are a delight to explore.

RUSTHALL
1½ miles W of Royal Tunbridge Wells off the A264

Although Rusthall lies on the outskirts of Royal Tunbridge Wells it has managed to retain some of its original rural character and not become completely engulfed by its much larger neighbour. A lovely common marks the heart of the village and some of the unusual rock structures that can be found in Royal Tunbridge Wells can also be seen here, in particular, there is **Toad Rock**, a local landmark.

SPELDHURST
2½ miles NW of Royal Tunbridge Wells off the A26

This attractive chiefly residential village was mentioned as early as the 8th century and, though close to Royal Tunbridge Wells, still manages to preserve a cohesive sense of village identity and a rural atmosphere. At its heart lies the village church that is built on the foundations of

MANOR COURT FARM

Ashurst, near Tunbridge Wells, Kent TN3 9TB
Tel: 01892 740279
Fax: 01892 740919

Found in a delightful Kentish village **Manor Court Farm** is a wonderful Georgian farmhouse that dates from 1740. Though a large and impressive building, the house also has a comfortable and relaxed atmosphere that extends from the exterior view right through to the splendid hospitality that is offered at this exceptional bed and breakfast establishment.

Run by Becky Masey, this glorious house has three superb guest rooms that are not only spacious but also provide everything that anyone staying here could possibly want - including a glorious view over the surrounding countryside. A full English breakfast is served to guests in the sunny dining room, which overlooks the garden, and, when available, fresh eggs are on the menu. The delightful country garden is just the place to relax in the early evening whilst, when the weather is too cold, there is an attractive guests' lounge complete with roaring fire. Guests at the farmhouse are very well cared for and the splendid countryside around Manor Court Farm can also be enjoyed by campers and caravanners who take advantage of the farm's camp site facilities.

THE GEORGE HOTEL

Stone Street, Cranbrook, Kent TN17 3HE
Tel: 01580 713348 Fax: 01580 715532

The George Hotel, Cranbrook, incorporating two bars, two restaurants and the hotel itself, offers style and elegance in the heart of Kent. The earliest part of this distinctive building dates back to 1290. Originally timber framed, it was given a new façade in the 18th century and it is reputed that King Edward I stayed here, as did Elizabeth I. This Grade II* Listed hotel has many traditional features such as the beamed ceilings, inglenook fireplaces and imposing 15th century oak staircase. There are said to be resident ghosts, including that of a Red Setter.

Graciously furnished and decorated throughout, the guests' lounge features handsome leather Chesterfield sofas, and the seven ensuite guest bedrooms are all well equipped - some have four poster beds, including one which is a replica of a Stuart bed found in Chatsworth House. The attractive and comfortable bars offer a fine range of beers, wines and spirits, including changing guest ales.

The hotel's elegant restaurant, 'brook's', has as its centrepiece a magnificent 15th century fireplace, once the busy hub of activity in the one-time kitchen - the open hearth has been beautifully preserved. In these refined surroundings, the menu boasts distinctly gourmet cooking. Dishes such as fillet of sea bass, peppered duck breast and hay baked lamb, as well as a mouth-watering variety of French cheeses and desserts including hot chocolate fondant with pistachio ice cream or old English regency syllabub with shortbread - and much more to tempt the palate - are complemented by a superb wine list. An alternative to this restaurant is an extensive bar menu available in the wine bar or lounge. Owners Sue and Douglas and their friendly, helpful staff offer a high standard of service and quality, ensuring guests a most enjoyable visit.

THE WHITE COTTAGE

Headcorn Road, Hawkenbury,
near Staplehurst, Kent TN12 0DU
Tel: 01590 892554 (day)
Tel: 01580 891480(eve & weekend)
e-mail: batten.j@talk21.com
website: thewhitecottagebb.com

Found in the heart of the Kentish countryside, yet close to many of the area's famous historic attractions, **The White Cottage** is an idyllic place to stay whether on business or holiday.

Dating back to the 18th century, and originally thought to be two cottages, this delightful family home is spacious and stands within its own large, well established garden. John and Nola Batten have lived here since the mid 1970s and, since 1993, they have been offering quality bed and breakfast accommodation from this charming house. As well as the three comfortable guest rooms, that each have their own bath or shower room facilities, guests staying at White Cottage have their own attractive beamed lounge, complete with a log fire in the inglenook fireplace on colder evenings, and breakfast is served in the elegant dining room that overlooks the garden.

Along with the superb accommodation, guests staying at the cottage also receive a warm and friendly welcome that has people from all over the world returning to here whenever they are in the area. Finally, tennis fans, or anyone looking to work off their breakfast, will be glad to hear that there is a tennis court here for them to use.

a much older Norman church that was struck by lightning in 1791. Great care was taken by the Victorians when the church was rebuilt and it is worth visiting as its contains some colourful stained glass windows that were designed by Burne-Jones.

CRANBROOK

Originally a little hamlet lying in the hills close to the source of the River Crane, Cranbrook began to grow in the 11th century and, by the end of the 13th century, it was sufficiently well established to be granted a market charter by Edward I. However, it was the introduction of the wool weaving from Flanders, in the 14th century that really changed the town's fortunes and, for the next few centuries, Cranbrook prospered. Several old buildings date back to this period of wealth and, along with the church and the Cloth Halls, there are winding streets lined with

Cranbrook Windmill

weatherboarded houses and shops. However, the industry began to decline and, by the 17th century, agriculture had taken over and, like other Wealden places, Cranbrook was transformed into a market town serving the needs of the surrounding area.

Often dubbed the 'Capital of the Kentish Weald', one of the best places to start any exploration of the town is at the **Cranbrook Museum** that is housed in a museum piece itself. Dating back to 1480, the museum is a fine example of a timber-framed building that is held together by elaborate joints. Opened in 1974, the displays and exhibitions here cover many aspects of Wealden life, from agriculture and local crafts to Victorian and wartime memorabilia. Naturally the town's reliance on the weaving industry is highlighted and, along with the collection of prints by the 19th century Cranbrook colony of artists, there is a display of local birds, many of which are now rare.

The parish church, **St Dunstan's**, is believed to have been built on the site of first a Saxon and then a Norman church. Locally known as the 'Cathedral of the Weald' and built between the 14th and the 16th centuries, this church, by its size, reflects the prosperity of the town at the time. Above the porch, and reached by a stone staircase, is a room known as 'Baker's Jail' where, in the reign of Mary Tudor, 'Bloody' Baker incarcerated Protestants he had convicted before they were executed. Originally, the room was intended to hold church valuables.

Whilst St Dunstan's church tower is tall the town is dominated by **Union Mill**, a very prominent local landmark that, at around 70 feet high, is the tallest smock mill in England. Built in 1814, the windmill was restored in the 1960s and, wind permitting, it still grinds corn into the flour that is sold here.

AROUND CRANBROOK

SISSINGHURST
1½ miles NW of Cranbrook on the A262

The main street of this village is lined with old weatherboarded houses that have been built over a period of several centuries but, in particular, many of the larger houses were erected by prosperous weavers who worked in the thriving industry that was

introduced to Sissinghurst during the reign of Edward III.

Sissinghurst is, of course, famous for the lovely gardens that were the creation of the writer Vita Sackville-West and her husband Harold Nicholson. When, in 1930, the couple bought **Sissinghurst Castle** it was all but a ruin. The castle was

Sissinghurst Gardens

THE BULL AT BENENDEN,

The Street, Benenden, Kent TN17 4DE
Tel: 01580 240054 e-mail: thebullatbenenden@btinternet.com
website: www.thebullatbenenden@btinternet.co.uk

Situated next to the village green, **The Bull at Benenden** is a delightful Grade II listed building that dates from 1608. With peg tiling that is typical of Kent and its unusual chinoiserie front windows, that date from the 19th century, this inn certainly easy to spot and, for the keen eyed, the pub sign has a different picture on each side - cricket bats on one, stumps on the other. This is a warm and friendly family run inn that offers its customers the very best in food, drink and hospitality and owners Caroline and Norman Pitt, along with their chocolate Labrador, Kahlua, have certainly made The Bull a popular place with both locals and visitors alike. Inside, the village bar is dominated by a massive inglenook fireplace and decorated with gleaming horse brasses whilst in the Cricket bar there is a display of memorabilia from the local club that includes a picture of the Queen Mother's visit in 1950. Attractive, comfortable and inviting throughout, including the separate dining room that

overlooks the village green, not only is this the place to come to for excellent drinks - there is always a selection of real ales and good wines at the bar - but The Bull has a growing reputation for the high standard of its cuisine. From light snacks through to a delicious three course dinner, chef, Paul Heather, creates a tasty and interesting array of dishes that are sure to tempt everyone. Popular at any time, booking is particularly advisable for the traditional Sunday roast lunches and the fish nights on Friday evening.

Sissinghurst Gardens

originally built in Tudor times by Sir John Baker, who, during the reign of Mary Tudor, sent so many Protestants to their deaths that he became known as 'Bloody' Baker. Such was Sir John's reputation that, so local legend tells when two women working at the castle heard him approaching they hid under the main staircase. From their hiding place they saw that their master was being followed by a servant carrying the body of a murdered woman and, as the men climbed the staircase, one of the dead woman's hands became caught in the banisters. Impatient to continue whatever gruesome tasks he was about to perform, Sir John quickly hacked the hand from the body and he and his servant continued up the stairs. Meanwhile, the severed hand fell into the lap of one of the women hiding below. Later, during the Seven Years War in the

18th century, the castle was used as a prison for 3,000 French troops and, by the time they had left, only a few parts of the original building were left standing. Decades of neglect and a short time as a workhouse finally saw the castle achieve the wrecked state of the 1930s.

Restoring what they could of the castle, the couple concentrated on creating the famous **Gardens** that, today, bring so much pleasure to visitors. Laid out in the Elizabethan style, there are a series of formal gardens, or 'rooms', that each have a different theme such as the White Garden where only silver leafed, white flowering plants are grown. Away from this formality there are woodland and lakeside walks and the estate's oast house is home to an interesting exhibition.

BENENDEN
3 miles SE of Cranbrook on the B2086

This attractive village, that is strung out along a ridge, is famous for its girls' public school, also called **Benenden**, that is housed in a mock Elizabethan house dating from 1859 that can be found to the west of the village centre. However, Benenden village itself is also famous - for cricket - that is played on most summer evenings on the village's large green.

ROLVENDEN
5 miles SE of Cranbrook on the A28

Surrounded by orchards and hop fields, this large village stands on the eastern fringe of the Weald and on the edge of the Isle of Oxney. A place of white weatherboarded and tile hung houses, the village is home to the **CM Booth Collection of Historic Vehicles**, that is chiefly centred on a unique collection of Morgan three-wheeled cars that date from 1913 to 1935. However, there is much more to discover at this fascinating museum, such as a 1904 Humber Tricar, numerous bicycles and motorcycles, toy and model cars and a whole host of other motorcar related memorabilia.

Close to the village lies **Great Maytham Hall** a charming country house that stands in glorious grounds. At the turn of the 20th century, the novelist Frances Hodgson Burnett, who spent most of her life in America, leased the house and, whilst staying here, she fell in love with the particularly beautiful walled kitchen garden that was to inspire her to write the classic children's book *The Secret Garden*.

SANDHURST
5 miles S of Cranbrook on the A268

Visitors coming here expecting to find the Royal Military Academy will be disappointed as this is located at Sandhurst, Berkshire. However, Sandhurst, Kent, is an attractive place that deserves a visit in its own right. Set in reasonably hilly terrain this feature of the countryside gave rise to the name of the local inn, The Missing Link, as it refers to the practice of linking extra horses to the wagons in order to pull heavy loads up the hill.

HERONDEN BARN

Rye Road, Sandhurst, Kent TN18 5PH
Tel:01580 850809 www: heronden.co.uk
e-mail: hdj@hdjohns.idps.co.uk
Heronden Barn offers luxurious bed and breakfast accommodation in a beautifully restored Kentish barn enjoying far-reaching views across The Weald, in the heart of the Garden of England. A warm welcome is extended to all visitors by the owners Ruth and Howard Johnson, who have lived in the house for nine years. They are a charming couple and like nothing more than looking after their guests and ensuring they have a pleasant stay.

The barn is around 400 years old, once forming part of a Kentish homestead, and many period features have been retained both inside and out while providing spacious and comfortable accommodation with plenty of character. Heronden Barn provides a comfortable and relaxing

environment that will appeal to a variety of people - young and old, independent travellers and families - for a short break or longer stay.

There are two large double bedrooms both with en-suite facilities and a single room with an extra settee bed, all of which have views over the gardens and surrounding countryside. Guests can use the downstairs lounge area for relaxing , planning their activities or watching the TV. Breakfast is served at times to suit individual guests and can be either Continental style, or traditional English. Although no evening meals are available, there are a number of nearby eating establishments.

List of Tourist Information Centres

ASHFORD TIC

18 The Churchyard, Ashford,
Kent TN23 1QG
Tel: (01233) 629165   Fax (01233) 639166

BROADSTAIRS TIC

6B High Street, Broadstairs, Kent CT10 1LH
Tel: (01843) 862242   Fax: (01843) 865650

CANTERBURY TIC

34 St Margaret's Street, Canterbury,
Kent CT1 2TG
Tel: (01227) 766567   Fax: (01227) 459840

CLACKET LANE (EASTBOUND) TIC

M25 Motorway Services, Junction 5-6,
Westerham, Kent TN16 2ER
Tel: (01959) 565063   Fax: (01959) 565064

CLACKET LANE (WESTBOUND) TIC

M25 Motorway Services, Junction 5-6,
Westerham, Kent TN16 2ER
Tel: (01959) 565615   Fax: (01959) 565617

CRANBROOK TIC

Vestry Hall, Stone Street, Cranbrook,
Kent TN17 3HA
Tel: (01580) 712538
Summer months only

DEAL TIC

Town Hall, High Street, Deal,
Kent CT14 6BB
Tel: (01304) 369576   Fax: (01304) 380641

DOVER TIC

Townwall Street, Dover, Kent CT16 1JR
Tel: (01304) 205108   Fax: (01304) 225498

EDENBRIDGE TIC

Stangrove Park, Edenbridge, Kent TN8 5LU
Tel: (01732) 868110   Fax: (01732) 868114

FAVERSHAM TIC

Fleur De Lis Heritage Centre,
13 Preston Street, Faversham,
Kent ME13 8NS
Tel: (01795) 534542

FOLKESTONE TIC

Harbour Street, Folkestone, Kent CT20 1QN
Tel: (01303) 258594   Fax: (01303) 259754

GRAVESEND TIC

10 Parrock Street, Gravesend,
Kent DA12 1ET
Tel: (01474) 337600   Fax: (01474) 337601

HERNE BAY TIC

12 William Street, Herne Bay, Kent CT6 5EJ
Tel: (01227) 361911

HYTHE TIC

En Route Building, Red Lion Square, Hythe,
Kent CT21 5AU
Tel: (01303) 267799, Fax: (01303) 260085
Summer months only

MAIDSTONE TIC

The Gatehouse, The Old Palace Gardens,
Mill Street, Maidstone, Kent ME15 6YE
Tel: (01622) 602169   Fax: (01622) 673581

MAIDSTONE M20 TIC

Motorway Service Area, Junction 8 M20,
Hollingbourne, Kent ME17 1SS
Tel: (01622) 602169   Fax: (01622) 738985

MARGATE TIC

22 High Street, Margate, Kent CT9 1DS
Tel: (01843) 220241   Fax: (01843) 230099

NEW ROMNEY TIC

Magpies, Church Approach, New Romney,
Kent TN28 8QT
Tel: (01797) 364044   Fax: (01797) 364194
Summer months only

RAMSGATE TIC

19-21 Harbour Street, Ramsgate,
Kent CT11 8HA
Tel: (01843) 583333   Fax: (01843) 591086

ROCHESTER TIC

95 High Street, Rochester, Kent ME1 1LX
Tel: (01634) 843666   Fax: (01634) 847891

SANDWICH TIC

Guildhall, Sandwich, Kent CT13 9AH
Tel/Fax: (01304) 613565

SEVENOAKS TIC

Buckhurst Lane, Sevenoaks, Kent TN13 1LQ
Tel: (01732) 450305   Fax: (01732) 461959

SWANLEY TIC

Swanley Branch Library, London Road,
Swanley, Kent BR8 7AE
Tel: (01322) 614660

TENTERDEN TIC

Town Hall, High Street, Tenterden,
Kent TN30 6AN
Tel: (01580) 763572   Fax: (01580) 766863
Summer months only

TONBRIDGE TIC

Tonbridge Castle, Castle Street, Tonbridge,
Kent TN9 1BG
Tel: (01732) 770929   Fax: (01732) 770449

TUNBRIDGE WELLS TIC

The Old Fish Market, The Pantiles,
Royal Tunbridge Wells, Kent TN2 5TN
Tel: (01892) 515675   Fax: (01892) 534660

WHITSTABLE TIC

7 Oxford Street, Whitstable, Kent CT5 1DB
Tel/Fax: (01227) 275482

Index of Towns, Villages and Places of Interest

List of Advertisers

R

S

T

U

V

W

Y

Hidden Places Order Form

To order any of our publications just fill in the payment details below and complete the order form *overleaf*. For orders of less than 4 copies please add £1 per book for postage and packing. Orders over 4 copies are P & P free.

Please Complete Either:

I enclose a cheque for £ [   ] made payable to Travel Publishing Ltd

Or:

Card No: [   ]

Expiry Date: [   ]

Signature: [   ]

NAME: [   ]

ADDRESS: [   ]

POSTCODE: [   ]

TEL NO: [   ]

Please either send or telephone your order to:

Travel Publishing Ltd   Tel : 0118 981 7777
7a Apollo House   Fax: 0118 982 0077
Calleva Park
Aldermaston
Berks, RG7 8TN

	PRICE	QUANTITY	VALUE

Hidden Places Regional Titles

	PRICE	QUANTITY	VALUE
Cambs & Lincolnshire	£7.99	....	....
Chilterns	£8.99	....	....
Cornwall	£8.99	....	....
Derbyshire	£7.99	....	....
Devon	£8.99	....	....
Dorset, Hants & Isle of Wight	£8.99	....	....
East Anglia	£8.99	....	....
Gloucestershire & Wiltshire	£7.99	....	....
Heart of England	£7.99	....	....
Hereford, Worcs & Shropshire	£7.99	....	....
Highlands & Islands	£7.99	....	....
Kent	£8.99	....	....
Lake District & Cumbria	£8.99	....	....
Lancashire & Cheshire	£8.99	....	....
Lincolnshire	£8.99	....	....
Northumberland & Durham	£8.99	....	....
Somerset	£7.99	....	....
Sussex	£7.99	....	....
Thames Valley	£7.99	....	....
Yorkshire	£7.99	....	....

Hidden Places National Titles

	PRICE	QUANTITY	VALUE
England	£9.99	....	....
Ireland	£9.99	....	....
Scotland	£9.99	....	....
Wales	£9.99	....	....

Hidden Inns Titles

	PRICE	QUANTITY	VALUE
South	£5.99	....	....
South East	£5.99	....	....
South and Central Scotland	£5.99	....	....
Wales	£5.99	....	....
Welsh Borders	£5.99	....	....
West Country	£5.99	....	....

For orders of less than 4 copies please add £1 per book for postage & packing. Orders over 4 copies P & P free.

Hidden Places Reader Reaction

The *Hidden Places* research team would like to receive reader's comments on any visitor attractions or places reviewed in the book and also recommendations for suitable entries to be included in the next edition. This will help ensure that the *Hidden Places* series continues to provide its readers with useful information on the more interesting, unusual or unique features of each attraction or place ensuring that their stay in the local area is an enjoyable and stimulating experience. To provide your comments or recommendations would you please complete the forms below and overleaf as indicated and send to:

> The Research Department, Travel Publishing Ltd,
> 7a Apollo House, Calleva Park, Aldermaston, Reading, RG7 8TN.

Your Name:

Your Address:

Your Telephone Number:

Please tick as appropriate: Comments ☐   Recommendation ☐

Name of *"Hidden Place"*:

Address:

Telephone Number:

Name of Contact:

Hidden Places Reader Reaction

Comment or Reason for Recommendation:

....

....

....

....

....

....

....

....

....

....

....